FOLLOW
Finding Hope: Faith for the Frustrated

Michael S. Rogers

WORDS MATTER
P U B L I S H I N G
OUR WORDS CHANGE THE WORLD

ISBN: 978-1-962467-24-7

Library of Congress Catalog Card Number: 2024935198

Dedication

For Artie and Drake, two men at each end of
my ministry who helped by their questions
to shape how I share my faith.

Acknowledgments

Many thanks to Patrick Lightfoot and Clint Burns, the two leaders of my cohort in the Bonhoeffer Project, for being the first to propose this idea was bigger than a blog post. I'd be remiss if I didn't also include my readers Paul Vanderveer, Mary Calhoun, Denise Savage, and Tammy Scott.

Table of Contents

PART 3: LIVE

Introduction

I'm not sure how it started, but when my kids were younger and wouldn't get to their chores right away, I would remind them, "Sooner started, sooner done." One time my youngest was dragging his feet and I started to get on him and he replied, "I know, I know; faster started, sooner over."

Sometimes, when you say something that seems perfectly clear to you, the one receiving gets a different message. Even if it's close, even if it's funnier, it isn't exactly what you are trying to say. That's a communication problem.

I believe the church has been suffering from the same. We've become so used to the message we received, tacking on our experiences that stem from the message, that we came up with a little different understanding of what our Messenger was saying.

This series is an attempt to reclaim the beauty and the power of the original message, even though I know I can never top what was already written in Scripture. But maybe I can help us rediscover the true intent in those letters and histories and prophecies. God has helped me rediscover my first love (Revelation 2:4). Not that I abandoned it, but that I had allowed it to morph into something different. My path started with a spiritual epiphany.

I shared it in the first volume, where we tackled our frustration and asked ourselves to repent of (rethink) using our frustration as motivation. We learned to wait, pray, and respond as God directs and not as our own judgment dictates. I hope that was as cleansing for you as it was for me.

That volume spoke into our faith, which was the first on my list of frustrations with myself and other believers. More needs to be said, but to uncover it we need to spend time on something more important. The Gospel.

Honestly, that's where I started. The teaching section of this volume was the catalyst for this entire series. I was working with a group of pastors on understanding the Good News and felt like I couldn't get it focused. The Gospel, right? How can a pastor not know what that is? Maybe I could pretend and say I was crafting an explanation of the Gospel that could be understood by churchgoers.

That would be a little true, but mostly dishonest. After fifteen years in ministry and thirty years as a Christian, I was once again trying to understand what the Good News is. I felt unfocused as I learned new ways of looking at it. Whenever I find myself in that spot, I know the best thing I can do is write it down to explain it to someone else.

One afternoon, I created a blog post that was over 4,000 words. The two men leading our cohort agreed to read it and give their thoughts. Both gave me great feedback, but the most helpful was that this article was too long for a blog post. Maybe too long for a magazine article. I read it again and realized I had started in the middle anyway.

The first volume, *Rethink*, came about so that I could get to this volume. Writing a challenging love letter to the church was not a new concept to me. I've been trying to organize my thoughts and convert them into a book for about ten years, but every effort seemed too snarky, too smart, too witty by half.

I've read books like that and hated them. Why would I write one? Yet I couldn't avoid the trap. Regardless of my approach, my tone was the same. I asked God to help me understand my problem and He made me aware of the root of it.

Frustration. I couldn't write what He had shown me because my motivation was my frustration—with Him, with myself, with the church, with the world. I asked God what I should do about it one morning as I prayed.

This doesn't happen often, but I received a one-word response I couldn't deny was from God: repent. What I could do to start this journey is rethink how I handled my frustration. To be honest, my first thought was, "Is there someone else up there with an idea?"

I knew, though. No one else up there, and no other answer. I suddenly saw how often I hurt the reputation of the church by my frustrated rants. No wonder I couldn't find a different voice. After much deliberation, kicking, and screaming, I repented of my use of frustration as my main motivation. Then I changed my focus. Instead of writing from my frustrated self, I decided to write *to* my frustrated self.

Rethink was as much about God dealing with me as it was trying to help you.

In case you missed the first volume or don't remember, I listed seven frustrations I have with Christianity in America. They are:

1. My faith
2. My salvation
3. Church members
4. The Church
5. The world
6. Evangelism
7. Understanding the Spirit

Instead of dealing specifically with one of these topics, God showed me I first had to deal with the frustration itself. As I did, I also recognized how my emotional state was affecting my faith. First, I had to stop trying to be God's judge of the church. Now, I can concentrate on my faith in earnest.

Going through that process cleared my mind to come back to the original issue. What is the Gospel? Why is it so hard to share sometimes? What have we done to make it easier to understand? Did we make it too easy? This is the most important issue we can discuss.

Don't get me wrong, what we shared together if you read *Rethink* was necessary. Had to come first for those of us who already believe. But it was not the most important. What made it helpful was that it cleared our minds some so we could tackle this issue. We're in a different frame of mind now.

If you haven't read it, that's okay, because the Gospel is the real starting place. Come into this volume with a willingness to see the teaching of Jesus with fresh eyes. A friend already or a new friend come lately, I pray for you what I prayed to God for me as I started this journey.

I do not cease to give thanks for you, remembering you in my prayers, that the God of our Lord Jesus Christ, the Father of glory, may give you the Spirit of wisdom and of revelation in the knowledge of Him...

— *Ephesians 1:16-17*

MAYBE THIS SEEMS TOO FUNDAMENTAL

You picked up the book, so you are at least standing in the aisle of a bookstore or curled up with a tablet or phone reading the preview pages. You're flying through the first section wondering if it's worth the purchase. Find out it's about The Gospel and you might be tempted to think, "I don't know. I think I've got that down."

I get it. Thought so, too. Until someone questioned my understanding, and I had the courage to look at it again. This far into my own ministry, this long in my own faith, I figured I'd go through this just to get to the next thing. The challenges

I encountered forced me to decide if I was willing to pray to God and trust Him to show me,

> ...*having the eyes of your heart enlightened, that you may know what is the hope to which He has called you, what are the riches of His glorious inheritance in the saints...*
> — *Ephesians 1:18*

I needed to start at square one to understand what God was building in me, and what He could build through me.

"CROSS" COUNTRY

Before I entered high school, I was diagnosed with Osgood-Slaughter disease in my left knee. No reason to explain the condition; suffice it to say my parents were advised to end my football career. My favorite sport was basketball, so that was okay; but that meant I had to find some way to stay in shape the first few months of the year.

Someone suggested I run cross country, a crazy sport where the normal punishment for mistakes in basketball is the whole sport: we ran. I took it up for the sole purpose of staying healthy so I could make the team in the winter.

I fell in love with it. Two great things about cross country. First, the competition is just as stiff. Second, the companion-ship within my team and with the other teams was closer than anything I'd ever experienced. We were trying to beat the other team, but if somebody went down everyone was concerned. After we finished a race, we would stand at the finish line and clap for slower guys from the other teams!

Our school was small and our chances of winning a meet were slim, so we adopted a vision statement from *The Blues Brothers* (a 1980 comedy). We wanted to get t-shirts with it emblazoned on the back, but our coach wouldn't let us. Can you imagine a bunch of high schoolers running around with bright letters on their backs proclaiming, "We're on a mission from Gyad!"

Yeah, God, but the way the character says it in the film is hilarious.

We figured if we couldn't win, we could determine who did. Instead of trying to pick off the top two runners of a team, we worked hard to place our first two runners ahead of that team's third runner, hurting their score. A bunch of losers having fun helping someone else lose.

In my junior year, though, something changed. A guy joined the team who was good, really good. Like top three in every meet good. It mattered suddenly if we were competitive because cross country is a team sport and our scores had to support his. So, we asked him what his secret was.

Unsurprisingly, it was practice. *Off-season* practice. He ran every day through the year so that when it came time for the season, all he had to work on was technique, strategy, and sprint. His stamina was built-in.

We went back to being losers who make others lose.

Here's my point. The Gospel is an off-season practice that prepares us for whatever else we do. We can't skip it and hope we can fake it at crunch time. We need to understand it so well that when the time comes to share it all we need to worry about is technique, strategy, and sprint.

This is not too fundamental for us. This is too important to skip. This is Cross country. The Gospel will cure our frustration about our faith and our salvation. So, buy the book already, and come running with me.

A QUICK NOTE

I haven't completed this book yet, but I already know one thing and suspect another.

I know we'll use the same format we did in *Rethink*. Know the tension and teaching. Be the person who believes and becomes. Live what you learn through your heart, soul, mind, and strength. Every volume will follow this structure.

I suspect that I may repeat myself. Get used to that throughout the seven volumes. In my life, I find the lessons that stuck with me were the ones I heard in different ways at different times until they clicked. Even if something I wrote in the first volume hits home for you, don't skip it if I talk about the same issue differently in this volume. Knowing a second way to share something means you will have more tools to reach more people.

Are you ready to get started?

Those who are Not Yet Believers pay close attention. You may have had the Gospel shared with you before and it wasn't all this. Maybe someone paid for you to read this thing because it meant something to them. Maybe you picked it up on your own. Either way, thank you. My hope is that by the next volume, you will be one of them. . .

Already Believers, you've had the Gospel shared with you before. For some of you, it wasn't all this. Don't make any rash judgments as you walk through these pages with me. Instead, hear the words of your Savior:

> *But blessed are your eyes, for they see, and your ears, for they hear. For truly, I say to you, many prophets and righteous people longed to see what you see, and did not see it, and to hear what you hear, and did not hear it.*
> — *Matthew 13:16-17*

Here's the first repeat:

> Pray for an open mind.
> Listen for God's heart.
> Let peace settle in your soul.
> And rise, Believer. Your King still reigns.

PART 1

KNOW

TENSION:
Know Jesus, No Peace

When I was still attending church just to make my girl-friend's mother like me, I met this guy named Mack Slocum. He was an older man who always wore a suit and I was a young punk who always wore my don't-touch-me clothes. I still don't know what caused him to take an interest in me.

Every week, her mom and dad would drag us to their Sunday School class. They had decent coffee and it wasn't boring, so I didn't mind going. Mack would meet me at the door or sidle up to me by the coffee pot and make conversation. When I took an interest in understanding who Jesus was, he was the first to notice the change.

One Sunday, he asked what I was learning. I told him I didn't really know, mostly because I didn't want to talk to him. He looked me in the eye and said he'd like to help me decide if all this Jesus stuff was true or not. To my surprise, I discovered I really wanted to know. I asked him how he could do that.

I'm tempted to quote him, but I don't remember the conversation in that kind of detail. What's important is that he showed me First John—a pretty short letter, only five chapters. He challenged me to engage with it in a very specific way. Read chapters one and two on Monday, two and three on Tuesday, three and four on Wednesday, four and five on Thursday, and the whole book on Friday. Then, on Sunday, he would ask me what I'd learned.

Crazy, I know, but I did it. The following Sunday, he met me before class and asked what I had learned. He thanked me for really doing it, complimented my observations, and then asked me to do it again the following week. I did. Every week. For three months.

At the end of those three months, I was sitting in the sanctuary of Southeast Christian Church in Louisville, Kentucky. Bob Russell was preaching and, as usual, gave an invitation to come forward for prayer or to make a decision for Jesus. I don't remember what he talked about that day. I only remember standing up.

My girlfriend had her arms around my elbow and as I stood, she pulled me back down. I stood up so forcefully that I pulled her out of her chair. She came with me. We went down front and let someone pray for us, then were led into a "decision room" where someone explained the Gospel to me using something called The Bridge illustration.

You're over here and God's over there. Sin makes a gap between you. The cross bridges the gap. Believe in Jesus and you will cross the gap to be on God's side. That's not exactly how it was presented, and this is a coarse description of it, but that's what I heard ("Faster started, sooner over").

We prayed for Jesus to save us and scheduled a time to be baptized. I remember going down under the water and being held there for a moment to signify the death of my old self. The really cool part, though, was when the pastor brought me back up. I could feel every little drop as they took turns sliding across my cheeks until I broke the surface and felt a cool, chill waft of air across my face.

Literally, I felt as if all my old self had been washed away into that pool and I had come up a completely new man. At the ripe age of 21, I felt like I had been given a second chance. Alcoholism was behind me. Doubt was behind me. All the terrible things I regretted lay dissolved in the water as I stepped into a new life.

I was painting houses with my dad then. Excited about my new faith, I would run a brush along some baseboard as I told the guy working with me all about Jesus. Sometimes, in midsentence, I looked up and realized I was the only person in the room. Undaunted, I would look for another chance later.

On Sundays, I found a class for younger adults and started attending. They mentioned the church had a whole curriculum about my new religion. In about two years, I took almost everything they offered. Everything from "The Books of the Bible" to "Revelation" fascinated me. When they couldn't offer me more, I went to Bible college in Cincinnati just to learn more about the Word of God.

But I struggled still. I learned finances from the culture of poverty and put myself in bad situations all the time. Alcohol still occasionally caught up with me. I still didn't know how to treat a woman with respect. My private life was riddled with secret sins. I dropped out of school.

Within just a few years, the cleansing of a second chance felt distant and unattainable. What had I done wrong?

DISCIPLED TO SIT AND LEARN

Fast forward a few years, and I was married to a beautiful girl and working at a credit union as a teller. We were quickly expecting our firstborn and I freaked out at about month seven. How were we going to afford this? I'd made so many bad decisions, I couldn't see my way out.

We didn't pray about it, didn't seek counsel. I just went to my boss and challenged her to let me be a loan officer. She agreed and the raise made me feel that I had avoided the trap. I hadn't. Financially, we were falling apart. Relationally, my wife and I were fighting more than making up.

Church? Have you ever heard of couch potatoes? You know, the ones who just sit on the couch with snacks and a remote and flip through the channels while drool runs down their chins? Nowadays they binge-watch a series on one of the streaming networks, but you get the idea. Couch potatoes stay on the couch so long they grow roots there.

We were pew potatoes. That is, whenever we decided to show up. We would go to a church of our choosing, largely based on our personal preferences, and let them entertain us as we grew roots right there in the same pew. Still believing in Jesus, we were in no way an advantage to the Kingdom of God. As a matter of fact, we were a drain on it. We weren't growing in our faith. Peter wrote to warn us that if we didn't grow, we would die.

> *For if these qualities are yours and are increasing, they keep you from being ineffective or unfruitful in the knowledge of our Lord Jesus Christ. For whoever lacks these qualities is so nearsighted that he is blind, having forgotten that he was cleansed from his former sins.*
> *— 2 Peter 1:8-9*

What had changed?

Over the course of about five years, I had learned the equivalent of a bachelor's degree in my faith. The local church didn't have much else to teach me. Occasionally, a sermon would hit me between the eyes and make me wonder why I wasn't experiencing what the pastor was describing. Yet my life did not reflect the transformation I was promised.

Mack had taught me to study, classes had taught me to study, and college had taught me to study. I was more prepared than most believers. Hadn't I felt all my sins wash away in the pool? Maybe I needed to be baptized again!

Nope. I just needed a better understanding of the Gospel.

LEARNING MORE OR LESS

(What I'm about to share isn't a reflection on my first church, my school, or the churches I attended later. I used to think so, but after repenting (rethinking) my frustration as motivation, I realized the truth. It's a reflection of me. I was warned, mentored, served, taught, and encouraged to engage. Somehow, I still missed an important part of the Gospel. "Faster started, sooner over.")

Thinking back on my spiritual journey, I realize how much of my conversion was owed to the benefits I would get if I said yes. Eternal life. Forgiven sins. Gifts of the Spirit. Love, support, community. A mentor once told me, "You win them to what you win them with." If I was won to Jesus with all the benefits, guess what I expected?

Benefits!

What was my job after being saved? Learn as much about the benefits as possible. How could God help me get my finances straight? Will He help me win the lottery? What can He do to make me stop my habitual sins? Immediate removal of desire? How can I be a better husband, father, friend, man, or person?

Answers are in the Bible for all those questions. But they weren't the answers I sought. If God was that big and that caring, wouldn't He just make it all easy for me? After all, He promised all these benefits!

I kept studying and asking and begging and pleading. After all that time in the Scripture, I started feeling uncomfortable about some of the verses. They just didn't sound like benefits to me.

> *Now great crowds accompanied him, and he turned and said to them, "If anyone comes to me and does not hate his own father and mother and wife and children and brothers and sisters, yes, and even his own life, he cannot be my disciple."*
>
> — *Luke 14:25-26*

Pretty sure I remembered studying that one in college, but He can't really expect me to live up to that, right? What kind of God tells me to hate all my relatives?

> *Whoever does not bear his own cross and come after me cannot be my disciple.*
>
> — *Luke 14:27*

I was born nearly two thousand years after the cross, so I might know better what this means than those disciples who heard it the first time. The cross is shameful, sacrificial, public, and messy. What does that mean for me?

My learning wasn't enough. Jesus wasn't asking me to know something about Him. He was asking me to believe something about Him, to believe in Him, and then live it out. Faith was more than knowledge. James' words suddenly began to haunt me.

What good is it, my brothers, if someone says he has faith
but does not have works? Can that faith save him?
— *James 2:14*

Finally, God had my attention. I couldn't just say I be-lieved in Him. I had to show it. My response was to double down on all my efforts. We were no longer pew potatoes. I taught Sunday School, led small groups, created our church's first assimilation ministry (got people to serve at the church), became a deacon, and even preached some. At one point my wife and I were a part of eleven different ministries between us.

What I had learned had been good for me, but my re-sponse was to swing the pendulum to the other side. Before, I had a tepid faith. Now, I had a hurried, busy faith. Every sinful act caused even greater guilt than before. As a leader and inte-gral part of our church's mission, I felt more responsibility for my slips and my waywardness.

On top of that, the more engaged I became the more I was exposed to church politics. People disguised preferences with spiritual excuses or just thwarted what God was doing by choosing not to decide. I wanted to shake every leader.

And shake every member who chose to sit on the sidelines. Couldn't they see how hard I was trying? Didn't they know how important these ministries were? I taught some mean stuff dur-ing that time. Said some things that were intended to shame, not just guilt, those who were not engaged.

All those efforts only managed to increase my frustration. Was this all that following Jesus offered? Was I doomed to feel ashamed forever despite the grace He gave me? Was I expected to run full tilt while others sat on the sidelines? Was the church ever going to be healed of her corruption in leadership?

I've carried on like this for over a decade, with no relief in sight. When God called me into full-time ministry, I thought I would change everything. I didn't. Aaaaaah! Was I fighting a losing battle? Was this just the way of things? Had God ordained this so that the end times would come?

There's hope, fellow frustrated believers. If your experience is similar, I want to help by reminding you of the Gospel given to us from the first. In Romans, Paul says something interesting right in the first chapter that tips us off to the cure that can bring you peace, purify the church, and create dynamic leaders filled with godliness.

> *For I am not ashamed of the Gospel, for it is the power of God for salvation to everyone who believes, to the Jew first and also to the Greek. For in it the righteousness of God is revealed from faith for faith, as it is written, 'The righteous shall live by faith.'*
>
> — *Romans 1:16-17*

All this is so bad for some of you that reading the last few pages may have brought on some PTSD (Post-Traumatic Sanctuary Disorder). You're trying but feel like you're failing. You're in love with Jesus but can't stand the church. You're frustrated beyond belief and even after rethinking (repenting of) your view of the Bride of Christ, you still feel the ache of powerless-ness as you consider what to do.

The Gospel is the answer. I don't promise it. God does.

If you've had these feelings, I think any mature believer could commiserate. If you've responded in anger or irritation, it's because some of the Gospel has been lost in your frustra-tion. I love when Jesus sends out the Twelve for the first time in Matthew 10 and He gives them instructions. He tells them to go only to the Jews, that God will provide for them, and the power Jesus has for healing will be theirs. He tells them to go into town and look for people of peace and stay with them while they minister. Then He says,

> *And if the house is worthy, let your peace come upon it,*
> *but if it is not worthy, let your peace return to you.*
> — *Matthew 10:13*

FINDING PEACE

Peace in this passage does not mean a lack of conflict. Strong's concordance says the root of this word is *eirene* and generally means "wholeness." So, Jesus sends out His A-team and tells them He's going to take care of them, but the first thing He has given them is His peace. His wholeness. They've discovered some of it as they learned from Him.

Then Jesus says, "Share that wholeness with others. Some will listen. Tell them, share with them, guide them, prepare them for when I come. Some will not. I'll deal with them later. Don't let them steal the wholeness you already have."

Don't let the frustrations you feel steal the peace Jesus gave you. You know the one, the peace that passes all understanding. The wholeness you have that no one understands, the one that keeps you from being arrogant about it even as you show God's glory through it.

For that, you need to remember the Gospel of Peace.

I do, too.

TEACHING: Revisiting
The Basics

My best friend came over to help me move into a new apartment. The two rooms and bath sat behind an old convenience store and hadn't received much care. Messy, trashy, nasty. We cleaned the bathroom and then cleaned the floors. Excited about our progress, we decided to remove the seven layers of wallpaper on the walls and paint it.

The landlord loved us for it.

So, we worked for an entire Saturday getting rid of the wallpaper. When we were done, we sat in the dark on the step from my walk to the sidewalk and enjoyed the cool summer night. I think I went back into the kitchen to get us a couple of drinks. That's when I saw the floor.

Walking back out to the curb, I gave him his drink and said, "You know, we probably should have done the walls before we did the floors."

He smiled. "Ah, forethought."

We laughed about it, but it was painful. Standing on the other side of our efforts, we could see the correct order of things. Before that, though, we could only think of how nasty the once-cleaned floor was.

Sometimes, keeping the end in mind is helpful.

When it comes to the Gospel, though, starting with the end in mind clouds our vision of it. Because we know more than the disciples did about the resurrection, we have a hard time seeing the development of the Good News. Missing that natural process, we can accidentally change "Sooner started, sooner done" to "faster started, sooner over."

Will you consider it with me? Will you walk through the Scripture as if you are a disciple who doesn't know the end yet? As we do, will you shelve what you know of the Gospel and listen with new ears?

The exercise will do us good, so take a journey with me. We are headed to Ephesus, where Paul has had great influence and where he spent as much time as just about anywhere else in the trips recorded in Acts. We are looking at some passages that used to confuse me before I revisited the Gospel.

This sounds like I'm going against my own advice, but to understand the beginning we start near the end of Acts. As we travel, please be patient. Pray. Listen. Engage. Wait until the end to agree or disagree. You might be surprised, as I was. Let's catch up with some disciples of John the Baptist and another teacher who spent time in Ephesus and Corinth.

A GREAT TEACHER SHORT OF KNOWLEDGE

Now a Jew named Apollos, a native of Alexandria, came to Ephesus. He was an eloquent man, competent in the Scriptures. He had been instructed in the way of the Lord.
— *Acts 18:24-24*

Apollos has always fascinated me. He arrives on the scene from nowhere and leaves us in the next chapter heading into obscurity. Don't get me wrong—by Scriptural account, his contribution was instrumental in Ephesus and Corinth and most likely all of Achaia. He's important, but unless he wrote Hebrews, as some scholars believe, the reason for his inclusion has to do with what he got wrong, not what he did right.

According to Acts, he was a Jew from Alexandria in Egypt who had heard of Jesus and was teaching correctly about him. Later he would be so influential that some believers in Corinth announced themselves as his followers (I Corinthians 1:12). In Ephesus, though, we find he had one flaw.

And being fervent in spirit, he spoke and taught accurately the things concerning Jesus, though he knew only the baptism of John.

— *Acts 18:25*

Priscilla and Aquila had traveled to Ephesus with Paul and stayed there. They listened to this great teacher and realized he was missing something. Taking him aside, they taught him "the way of God more accurately" (Acts 18:26). What was he getting wrong? His learning was based on John, not Jesus. When they corrected him, he immediately went to Achaia and wound up in Corinth.

Interestingly, Paul comes back on the scene in Acts 19 and passes through Ephesus shortly after Apollos left. He finds some disciples of Jesus and recognizes something is different.

> *And he (Paul) said to them, "Did you receive the Holy Spirit when you believed?" And they said, "No, we have not even heard that there is a Holy Spirit." And he said, "Into what then were you baptized?" they said, "Into John's baptism." And Paul said, "John baptized with the baptism of repentance, telling the people to believe in the one who was to come after him, that is, Jesus."*
>
> — *Acts 19:2-4, parenthesis mine*

Sounds like they got a lot of things right. They believed in Jesus, not John. They believed in repentance and were baptized. But Paul can still tell something is different and goes right to the problem. Disciples who happened to be in the place where Apollos was teaching and had heard only part of the Good News of Jesus had not even heard of the Holy Spirit. They knew only a baptism of repentance.

JOHN PREPARED THE WAY FOR JESUS

In John 1:19-28, the Baptist is asked if he is the Christ, and he says no. Then they ask if he is Elijah or a prophet. He says, "I am the one Isaiah warned you about. I am not him, but The Christ is among you now."

John appeared, baptizing in the wilderness and proclaiming a baptism of repentance for the forgiveness of sins.
                                        — *Mark 1:4.*

Even many Not Yets have heard of John the Baptist; many of the Already Believers do not completely understand his significance. John was sent to prepare the way for Christ. How did he do that? By preaching the very thing we often preach in the church today.

- **Repent** – rethink what you know about God, about yourself, about how to live your life. You've been going in one direction for a long time, and it has led you to do things you regret.
- **Sins** – the acts of people that hurt others and hurt themselves and, ultimately, hurt their relationship with God—the word most often used means "miss the mark." When I lie, I deceive someone for my own ends, but I also forfeit my integrity. At the same time, I put myself at odds with God.

- **Forgiveness** – So if I "rethink" my relationship with God, with others, and with myself, and I ask God to forgive me for those purposeful and accidental acts, then God is predisposed to grant me that grace.

This is, in effect, "John's Gospel." His Good News (the definition of the *gospel*) is that we need not remain imprisoned by our sins. We don't have to make amends; we just have to rethink our part in those hurtful deeds and ask God to forgive us.

This doesn't mean we could have stopped with John's version and done without Jesus. John was preparing the way, not presenting the way. Let that sink in. What John preached by itself was not enough. How does it line up with what we've heard preached today?

Then Jesus comes along after John has prepared the way and gives *His* Gospel:

Now after John was arrested, Jesus came into Galilee, proclaiming the Gospel of God, saying, "The time is fulfilled, and the Kingdom of God is at hand; repent and believe in the Gospel."

— *Mark 1:14-15*

Where John focused on the forgiveness of sins, Jesus focused on a different aim entirely. (For those of the Already who are getting nervous, bear with me until the end.)

- **The time is fulfilled**–God is ready to reveal His plan completely. In Eden, God created man and woman and gave them dominion under Him to rule the earth. They chose instead to rule it on their own. God's kingdom became, in a way, mankind's kingdom. Unwittingly, mankind put themselves under a different dominion, an enemy of God. Through their own desire to rule alone and the enemy's desire to thwart God, mankind suffered for centuries as they progressed, evolved, and still found themselves at the mercy of selfish rulers. No man-made government has been sustainable. Every time, the selfishness of individuals or groups becomes despotism and tyranny. We even see that in democracies. Jesus tells us He is ready to reveal His reign over the earth once and for all.

- **The Kingdom of God is at hand**–The reign of a king is not determined by boundaries but is limited to his influence on those who swear allegiance to him. Where the people are faithful, the king reigns. Otherwise, the king must either give up his right to rule them or resort to tyranny to get obedience from them. Jesus tells us the Kingdom of God—the influence of God, the reign of God—is at hand. I always like to think of Him holding His hands out and smiling at the physical reality of His statement. Those same hands, stretched out to include everyone, will be nailed to a cross to prove His deity and ask for our allegiance. No tyranny or despotism, just sacrifice.

- **Repent**–Check this out! He includes ALL of John's Gospel in this one word. He's not replacing the Good News John the Baptist was teaching; He's enhancing it, enlarging it, explaining it even more. John prepared the way for him. He is simply fulfilling His mission.
- **Believe**–oh, how this word has been abused. This does not mean "to give mental assent to a group of facts." The root of this word is much deeper. It speaks to a faith in something or someone that will dictate what that person does. Real faith provokes action.

Put it together and Jesus is teaching, from the very beginning, that the Good News is that God is making a way for His influence to spread as He commands allegiance to live a better life where sin is forgiven and life is better lived if we would just believe it enough to do it His way.

But where is the mention of Jesus living a perfect life, dying for our sins, and rising again on Easter morning? The disciples spend roughly two years with Him before He even mentions it. What causes Him to finally reveal the great plan?

Here John "prepares the way" again. Remember, he told them that Christ was among them. He also proclaimed something important right at the very beginning.

> *The next day he saw Jesus coming toward him and said, "Behold, the Lamb of God, who takes away the sin of the world!"*
>
> *— John 1:29*

32

The final elements of the Gospel are there, but the disciples are not ready to hear it yet. Jesus teaches them, lives with them, sweats with them, dances with them, cries with them first. He releases them and draws them back, celebrates their successes, and chastises their mistakes. Then, when the time is ripe, He opens up about how He will accomplish what John prophesied at the beginning.

> *And He asked them, "But who do you say that I am?" Peter answered Him, "You are the Christ." And He strictly charged them to tell no one about Him. And He began to teach them that the Son of Man must suffer many things and be rejected by the elders and the chief priests and the scribes and be killed, and after three days rise again.*
>
> *— Mark 8:29-31*

Not until the disciples finally realize that Jesus is the Christ and are willing to openly proclaim it does Jesus add the details of the way the Gospel would be enacted. "The Christ" is Greek for the Hebrew word, "Messiah." They both mean, "The Anointed One." We don't have to be Bible scholars to know that the Kings of Israel, especially Saul and David, were anointed as kings.

Once Jesus saw that His disciples understood Him as the Anointed One and gave their allegiance to Him, He reveals the way it would come about. Jesus would be falsely charged—necessarily since He lived a sinless life—mocked, beaten, and hung on a cross. He would be put in a grave where He would spend three days before proving Himself by rising again.

Jesus is going to spend another year with them and He's going to warn them at least twice more about what is coming. But here, when He has revealed the plan, what is most on His mind? After Peter tries to correct Him, Jesus rebukes him and turns to His disciples with a message.

> *"If anyone would come after Me, let him deny himself and take up his cross and follow Me. For whoever would save his life will lose it, but whoever loses his life for My sake and the Gospel's will save it."*
>
> — *Mark 8:34*

Discipling was His first thought. Following Him. Giving up everything for His sake. Giving up everything for the sake of the Good News.

John the Baptist came proclaiming a repentance Gospel. Jesus added to it His teaching about the Kingdom and following Him. If we go back to the first chapter of Mark, we even see it there. Right after Jesus starts proclaiming the Gospel of the Kingdom, He calls to Simon and Andrew:

> *And Jesus said to them, "Follow me, and I will make you become fishers of men."*
>
> — *Mark 1:17*

So, the elements of the Gospel of Jesus are:

1. The Kingdom of God is spreading God's influence.
2. Jesus is the anointed King and He reigns over the Kingdom of God.
3. So repent—rethink—how you live your life and ask for forgiveness.
4. And believe through His death and resurrection Jesus makes you clean and disciples you.
5. So, give your allegiance to Him, and follow Him to enlarge His kingdom by influencing others.

SHOUT OUT TO THE BONHOEFFER PROJECT

As I stated in the introduction, I was in a cohort with other pastors who explored what the Gospel is. I owe the emphasis of the Gospel of Jesus to Bill Hull's work in *Conversion and Discipleship*, a book I highly recommend. The cohort is part of The Bonhoeffer Project and I also highly recommend that process for any church leader who wants to raise up disciple-makers.

They got me thinking and I can't thank them enough for that. Gratitude, after all, is the only right response to such a gift. What follows is the best way I know to communicate what they urged me to explore. This is my own personal take. It involves three different versions of the Gospel available in the church today.

1. Grace-only: This includes the grace (repentance and forgiveness) of John the Baptist and the sacrifice of Jesus but skips the Kingdom.
2. Truth-only: This includes the sacrifice of Jesus and a kingdom but skips the grace (repentance and forgiveness) of John the Baptist.
3. Grace-and-Truth: This includes the grace (repentance and forgiveness) of John the Baptist, the sacrifice of Jesus, and allegiance to the Kingdom.

GRACE-ONLY VS. TRUTH-ONLY VS. GRACE-AND-TRUTH

Those invested in a Grace-Only Gospel rightly worry that this line of thinking will lead to a works-oriented religion. If salvation is not a free gift but requires obedience, then we have to ignore Paul when he says:

> *But God, being rich in mercy, because of the great love with which He loved us, even when we were dead in our trespasses, made us alive together with Christ—by grace you have been saved—and raised us up with Him and seated us with Him in the heavenly places in Christ Jesus…"*
> — *Ephesians 2:4-6*

Their misgivings are understandable, but I'm not talking about a works-oriented salvation. Already Believers know better than that. But we find it difficult to avoid tipping too far one way or the other when we live out grace and truth. Truth-only salvation says that even after we are saved we must act purely under God's law to stay saved. Grace-only teaches we are saved by grace through our faith in Christ Jesus but are not restricted any longer by God's law.

Very rarely do either of these Gospels operate in their purest form. Each Grace-only will have a nod to the truth, and each Truth-only will have a nod to grace. Some will give bigger nods than others. At the end of the day, however, the Grace-only Gospel will create consumer Christians and the Truth-only Gospel will create burned-out or judgmental Christians.

Grace-and-truth salvation agrees with Grace-only but questions our definition of faith. If faith is simply a mental assent to a list of facts, then the Gospel of Jesus is all about forgiveness. However, if faith is such trust in a person that one is willing to give allegiance to whatever that person says, then God is speaking of something greater than fire insurance or a ticket to heaven.

And I believe this is true. Grace is sufficient for our salvation and that is the Truth. Our faith that activates grace is a trust in a Savior on such a level that we give allegiance to Him as Lord. Yet we know, don't we, that no Christian is made perfect by the sinner's prayer or by dunking in water, or by a church-centered lifestyle.

Wouldn't it be great if the moment we swear allegiance to God we are transported in a shaft of light to the heavenly realms? We aren't, though. Why? Because the process by which

God makes us holy will prepare us for that eternity and at the same time will influence others. The Kingdom of God can't be expanded here by whisking the Already into heaven. The Not Yets have to see the Already live out the allegiance that saved them.

Here's more Good News: Grace and truth are sufficient to make us holy, too.

WHO IS TIRED OF TRYING SO HARD?

A man once told me he never wears Christian attire. He knows he is going to sin, and he doesn't want to misrepresent Jesus when he does. Rather than disappoint Jesus, he avoids any outward sign that he's a Christian.

But that's all backward, isn't it? Shouldn't wearing the t-shirt and being reminded of our allegiance to Christ prevent us from sinning? It's like trusting God for our salvation but not our sanctification. Sure, grace is sufficient for bringing me forgiveness; but can I also count on grace to help make me holy?

Didn't Paul struggle with this, too?

For I know that nothing good dwells in me, that is, in my flesh. For I have the desire to do what is right, but not the ability to carry it out. For I do not do the good I want, but the evil I do not want is what I keep on doing.
— *Romans 7:18-19*

Those who Already Believe use this verse often to shake their weary heads and say, "See? There's nothing we can do about it. Even Paul struggled as he continued to sin!"

A better look at this passage reveals a different meaning, however. Paul is not talking about his current life under the grace of Jesus Christ in this passage. He's describing what he escaped!

Paul spends the first third of this chapter of Romans reminding us that we are released from the law through the death and resurrection of Jesus. As he often does, he poses a question in verse seven that he imagines some will ask in light of this. Is the law a sin? No, the law is a mirror that helps us recognize our sins. It is not bad, it is holy. Despite this, the one thing the law can't do is transform someone. Instead, it produces sin in us.

For we know that the law is spiritual, but I am of the flesh, sold under sin.

— Romans 7:14

He speaks of himself here not as a Grace-and-truth-saved individual but of his state under the works-oriented law. It is spiritual; he is of the flesh. When he sees the holiness of the law, his will cannot long follow it. Something inside makes him do what he doesn't want to do and avoid doing the things he should do.

His point here is that the situation under the law is hopeless. We cannot work for our salvation. So, he laments and then celebrates.

Wretched man that I am! Who will deliver me from this body of death? Thanks be to God through Jesus Christ our Lord! So then, I myself serve the law of God with my mind, but with my flesh I serve the law of sin.
— *Romans 7:24-25*

The only thing that can save Paul from the conundrum under the law is Jesus! But what about that last sentence? He is realizing the helplessness he experiences on his own. His mind (where he makes choices) wants to follow the law of God, but his flesh won't allow it. What is the cure? How can he do what he promotes in another letter:

Therefore, my beloved, as you have always obeyed, so now, not only as in my presence but much more in my absence, work out your own salvation with fear and trembling…
— *Philippians 2:12*

REMEMBER WHAT JOHN'S BAPTISM WAS MISSING?

Let's go back to those passages in Acts.

And (Paul) said to them, "Did you receive the Holy Spirit when you believed?" And they said, "No, we have not even heard that there is a Holy Spirit."
— *Acts 19:2*

John the Baptist knew the difference from the beginning. After telling the priests and Levites he was not the Christ, they asked why he was baptizing them. He answers in an interesting way.

> *"I baptize you with water for repentance, but He who is coming after me is mightier than I, whose sandals I am not worthy to carry. He will baptize you with the Holy Spirit and fire."*
>
> — *Matthew 3:11*

Once again, John is preparing the way. Is it any wonder that Peter, who describes the Gospel of the church in his first sermon, tells the people what they must do to be saved:

> *And Peter said to them, "Repent and be baptized every one of you for the forgiveness of your sins and you will receive the gift of the Holy Spirit."*
>
> — *Acts 2:38*

Peter does not mention faith, but no honest theologian denies that repentance (rethinking) requires belief. What kind of belief? The allegiance kind. But what if we can't follow Jesus like that? What if we can't be holy as our heavenly Father is holy? It wouldn't be fair for God to expect us to follow in the footsteps of Jesus!

Unless, of course, He provides the power to follow. Let's go back to Romans.

There is therefore now no condemnation for those who are in Christ Jesus. For the law of the Spirit of life has set you free in Christ Jesus from the law of sin and death.

— Romans 8:1-2

We have received forgiveness and are no longer under the judgment of God based on our upholding of the Law. Salvation is by grace through our faith. We now have a new "law" and that is the power of the Spirit in us.

For God has done what the law, weakened by the flesh, could not do. By sending His own Son in the likeness of sinful flesh and for sin, He condemned sin in the flesh, in order that the righteous requirement of the law might be fulfilled in us, who walk not according to the flesh but according to the Spirit.

— Romans 8:3-4

Where before we couldn't be holy because we had to rely on our willpower and the instruction of the law, we are now able to be holy because we can walk in the Spirit and let Him help us choose life. The law could have saved us if our flesh would allow it, but it would not. We are rebels nearly from birth. We test our parents, we test the school system, we test law enforcement, we test our bosses, we test the establishment, we test God.

For God to save us by forgiving our sins and then leave us here to live under the law the rest of our lives would be a horrific divine bait and switch. That is not what God has done! His grace for salvation comes through Jesus Christ; His grace for sanctification comes through the Holy Spirit. How do we know we can trust that?

Because it is also True. Paul spends the rest of chapter eight in Romans explaining it, but here is the crux:

If the Spirit of Him who raised Jesus from the dead dwells in you, He who raised Christ Jesus from the dead will also give life to your mortal bodies through His Spirit who dwells in you.

— Romans 8:11

The root of the words that mean "give life" in this passage is *Zoe*, a Greek word that encompasses all your life. It is the same word Peter uses when he tells us...

His divine power has granted to you all things pertaining to life and godliness, through the knowledge of Him who called us to His own glory and excellence.

— 2 Peter 1:3

Jesus didn't save us to leave us wallowing in sin. His grace is the heart of His truth. He saved us and filled us with His Spirit to be holy and to be emptied for others! Remember that earlier passage from Philippians? Look how the sentence ends.

Therefore, my beloved, as you have always obeyed, so now, not only as in my presence but much more in my absence, work out your own salvation with fear and trembling, for it is God who works in you to will and to act in order to fulfill His good purpose.

— *Philippians 2:12*

How does God work in you? The Holy Spirit!

AN ACTIVE FAITH IS ABOUT ALLEGIANCE, NOT WORKS

If we read this passage with different eyes and hear it with different ears, we begin to understand that the Gospel is Grace-and-truth, not Grace-only or Truth-only. Now that you are attuned to this, listen to the words of James and hear his message to the Already:

What good is it, my brothers, if someone says he has faith but does not have works? Can that faith save him? If a brother or sister is poorly clothed and lacking in daily food, and one of you says to them, "Go in peace, be warmed and filled," without giving them the things needed for the body, what good is that? So also faith by itself, if it does not have works, is dead.

— *James 2:14-17.*

James is not arguing with Paul. He's not promoting a works-oriented or even a Truth-only salvation, although he is concerned about the salvation of some. Not because they don't believe in Christ, but because they have not given their faith to Christ. The Bible doesn't make a distinction between these two words—belief and faith—nor should it. We must, though, because of the promotion of a Grace-only Gospel that doesn't do the Gospel of Jesus adequate justice.

When we say we believe in Christ, we often mean we agree that the facts about Jesus are true. He was born of a virgin, lived a sinless life, died a horrible death, was buried, and rose again. All of this He did to save me from my sin. He is my Savior. That is grace.

But in our confession of faith, we say, "I believe that Jesus is the Christ, the Son of the Living God, my *Lord* and Savior."

Everything we mean when we say we believe in Christ is true, but it's not enough. We must also have faith in Christ to do as He commands. As our King, our Lord, our Christ, our Messiah, our Anointed One, the Son of God, we must give our allegiance to Him as well as our acknowledgment of His deeds.

To be a disciple once meant more than a student who agreed with the teaching of his Rabbi. Instead, the pupil wanted to think like him, speak like him, act like him, live like him, *smell like him* if he could. Why would we want to give less to the One who saved us from eternal destruction? He doesn't present a better way to live—He presents the *only* way to live well. Let's go back to Ephesians where we can see that Paul agrees with Peter and James.

> *For by grace, you have been saved through faith. And this is not your own doing; it is the gift of God, not as a result of works, so that no one may boast. For we are His workmanship, created in Christ Jesus for good works, which God prepared beforehand, that we should walk in them.*
> — *Ephesians 2:8-10*

If our allegiance isn't implied, why does Paul finish by pointing to the good works God prepared for us to do? What can we do about that?

THE LORDSHIP OF JESUS IS NOT OPTIONAL

John the Baptist exalts Christ above himself in John 3:22-36. In the same way, the Gospel of Jesus is exalted as He proves His divinity, conquers death and spreads His kingdom through His disciples.

Listen. If you are already a believer, you need to hear this even if it is painful. If you are Not Yet a believer, you need to know what it means to say yes to Jesus.

We don't have an option where Jesus saves us and we can go on about our sinful lives however we want. The calling of Christ is greater than that and the sacrifice of Christ deserves more than that. But the empowerment of Christ is greater than that, too. Our duty is to walk in the Spirit and live under the influence of our King where we advance the work of His Kingdom so that the Not Yet may recognize The Way.

Before it was called Christianity, followers of Jesus talked about The Way. Of course, it's a reference to Jesus saying, "I am the way, the truth, and the life…" (John 14:6), but it also speaks of a certain lifestyle. A way of living. A way through a narrow gate. A way of grace through faith in the Spirit.

A way to eternal life that starts right now.

There's more, because if walking in the Spirit is the key to holiness, then the Spirit is more important than we credit Him. But for the moment, let this definition of the Gospel sink in:

Good News! The Kingdom of Heaven is reclaiming earth through the life, death, and resurrection of Jesus Christ of Nazareth, God's only Son. We who repent of our sins and give allegiance to Him are forgiven and empowered by the Holy Spirit to spread His influence as we boldly follow in His footsteps.

This is the Gospel I have come to understand. This is the correction I believe Priscilla and Aquila gave to Apollos. This is why the disciples of John the Baptist had not heard of the Holy Spirit.

One last way to think of it. The Grace-only Gospel gives most of its weight to the benefits. The Truth-only Gospel gives most of its weight to the responsibilities. The Grace-and-Truth Gospel finds its fullness in Christ through a tension between the benefits and responsibilities.

For the law was given through Moses; grace and truth came through Jesus Christ.

— John 1:16

We have benefits and responsibilities in our response to the Gospel of Jesus Christ. If we lean too heavily one way or the other, we risk an adverse effect on the church. The healthy believer, the healthy church, will be full of Grace *and* full of Truth.

PART 2

BE

BELIEVE: How This Changes "Frustrated Me"

I know asking for directions is hard for a guy, but I do occasionally realize I need help getting somewhere. If the person at the gas station tells me how to get to my destination, I have a choice to make. I can listen and do exactly what he says, I can listen and decide which parts I want to follow, or I can choose not to listen at all. How I respond depends largely on whether I trust the one giving me directions.

But the point isn't that I get directions. The point is that I arrive at the destination.

Sometimes I really listen to the directions and intend to follow them, but something happens along the way. I misremember them (a guy's word that means he only *partially* forgot) or I see a potential faster way and make a judgment call. My wife calls the former forgetting and the latter my own personal shortcuts.

Almost always, no matter what we call them, we either get to the destination late or don't get there at all. I still argue that I

51

don't completely forget and that I don't completely distrust the person who gave me directions. I just forget the point.

Looking back on my experience, I realize I was one of the blessed ones. Mack discipled me almost from day one. The church I attended gave me all the information I needed. College, life, and the local church gave me a safe place to learn how to live as a servant of Jesus. Nothing in my spiritual upbringing made me misunderstand the Gospel.

I just misremembered and took some of my shortcuts.

When I was provided the benefits of the Gospel, I latched onto them like a drowning man to a passing raft. I needed salvation, not a new list of jobs to do. Had my understanding stopped there, I don't know where I'd be today. Fortunately, the people around me—even before I truly believed—were instilling in me the idea that Jesus was more than a ticket to heaven.

If you doubt me, read First John. A person can't read that book every week for three months and feel like they are just winning the spiritual lottery.

And by this we know that we have come to know Him, if we keep His commandments.

— 1 John 2:3

And now little children, abide in Him, so that when He appears we may have confidence and not shrink from Him in shame at His coming.

— 1 John 2:28

Little children, let us not love in word or talk but in deed and in truth.

— *1 John 3:18*

For this is the love of God, that we keep His commandments. And His commandments are not burdensome.

— *1 John 5:2*

I listed these originally as evidence, a random drawing from the letter to prove my point. But I also see a pattern in them (most likely because they appear in order!) and want you to see it, too.

- ■ Come to know Him in a way that moves you to allegiance, and you will obey His commandments. How can you keep those commandments?
- ■ Abide in Him. Take up residence in Him. Live in Him. That is only possible through the Holy Spirit who lives in us. What does that look like?
- ■ Love in deed and in truth. Don't just talk about how loving you are. Prove it by your everyday choices. How do we know what love is?
- ■ Go back to the beginning. Obey the commands of the One you're abiding in, the One who knows that grace is the heart of God's truth.

Had I been listening from the first, I would have known.

Maybe you've had the same experience, but maybe you haven't. Your world is rocked because someone sold you the Gospel on the benefits and now when they expect you to change you feel manipulated. I'm so sorry, brother. Forgive us, sister. But the destination is not salvation—that's just the real starting line.

The destination is holiness. The destination is godliness. The destination is eternal love.

Don't fret, though. God knows right where you are, and maybe that's why you picked up this book. Already Believers, as I spend a little time talking to the Not Yets, do me a favor. Listen in on our conversation. This isn't about your salvation—I believe God has saved you already—but the next section might help you understand that God has so much more for you.

So. Much. More.

FOR THOSE NOT YET BELIEVERS

Nowadays, it's hard to believe in anything. We've been told so many lies by our government, our political parties, our media, our experts, our friends, our family, and ourselves, we just aren't sure if anyone is authentic anymore. I can't imagine how difficult it is to face life unsure of what is dependable. It's like walking on a path that looks safe, but you're pretty sure it'll be quicksand any moment.

If only there was another way, right?

I believe the Grace-and-Truth Gospel of Jesus is the other way. The problem is, The Way has been so covered by American Christianity that you will have a hard time trusting this, too. I feel you. And if no one else from the church has said it to you yet, I'm sorry. I'm really, really sorry.

No, I take that back. "I'm sorry" can mean too many things. I'm sorry you caught us. I'm sorry you feel that way. I'm sorry you don't agree with us. I'm sorry you don't measure up. I'm sorry you don't think we measure up. "I'm sorry" isn't going to cut it, because in saying it I retain all the power. So let me give it up, as Jesus would ask me to do.

Please forgive us.

Now, the ball's in your court. You can decide whether to forgive us or not. We aren't absolved by your forgiveness, but your forgiveness will give me a chance to "show you a more excellent way" as Paul says in 1 Corinthians 12:31, the verse right before he describes godly love. If you can find it in your heart to forgive us, then please, read on.

FAITH, NOT BELIEF

Two conversations, two atheists, same result. They each were talking to me about God and trying to understand why I believe in Him. At the same time, they were explaining why they didn't believe. One of them used to believe in Jesus, the other had been around churches all his life but never believed in Jesus. Each one rallied around the same idea. "I'm just not a person of faith."

I had been learning about the Grace-and-Truth Gospel, so my first reaction was to ask a question. "What is faith?"

Sounds silly, doesn't it? Everyone knows what faith is. Don't they? Both of these men—one older, one younger, one a former believer, and one a lifelong atheist—had a long history with the church. They should give the church answer, right?

"What is faith?"

Without hesitating, both said, "Faith is believing without evidence."

I was offended. Here I am, not just a believer, a regular church attender, a leader in the church... I'm a pastor! I make a living off this religion, to be crass about it. And they think everything I've built my life around is based on believing in something without any evidence?

I'm not sure I handled either conversation deftly. The shock of it didn't wear off in time. Who did they think I was? I'd like to think I appear intelligent. Would a smart person just decide to believe something without evidence?

After recovering and praying, reasoning, and asking God, I realized this has been the root of many of the problems in the church. To understand it, I had to test it. Was this really what my faith was? A blind leap about something I couldn't prove?

In each case, the men in question had some exposure to me and knew me fairly well. I don't think either of them meant to insult my intelligence. So, what did they mean?

When they said evidence, they meant something tangible, seen, unmistakable. Something that happened *today*. Both had heard sermons and prayers and seen results or the lack of results. Both had been around church people and watched their lives. Both had asked themselves if there was any evidence that what we were saying was true.

They didn't care about the Scripture, didn't care about whether or not Jesus really existed, and didn't question the good that had come out of Christian missions, ministries, and benevolence. What they meant was they saw no proof *today* that God is real and that Jesus is trustworthy.

This isn't a new issue. Paul addresses it with the church in Corinth.

For Jews demand signs and Greeks seek wisdom, but we preach Christ crucified, a stumbling block for Jews and folly to the Gentiles, but to those who are called, both Jews and Greeks, Christ the power of God and the wisdom of God.

— 1 Corinthians 1:22

In his time, Paul realized the two groups of people who were deciding what to do about Jesus had different issues. He recognized the two were starting from different places. The Jews knew God was one and that He would send a Messiah. All they needed to decide was if the signs Jesus performed qualified Him as the Messiah. More confusing, Jesus had died without becoming King of Israel. How could He be the one? This was a great stumbling block for them.

The Greeks were more concerned about the teaching of Jesus. Could they swallow the idea that God is one? They'd lived under the concept of many gods for so long, it seemed too simple to believe in one. How could they differentiate this one God from the many? Wisdom, perhaps? They would look at what was said, taught, lived, and decide if it had enough merit to change. Where the Jews had to admit the many signs Jesus performed, the Greeks had to admit the wisdom of Jesus.

But one God? In the flesh? Who died and rose again to save us from our sins? Folly!

One was looking for a sign, the other for wisdom. Jesus offered the cross. The evidence they requested wasn't the evidence they got. Jesus didn't want the Jews to believe in the signs and He didn't want the Greeks to believe in the teaching. He wanted both to put their faith, their allegiance, in *Him*. Don't get me wrong: Jesus gave signs and wisdom enough. He just wanted something more from His followers.

What are my two friends seeking? To believe, they must see evidence today that it is real. How would they be convinced? By being present for a multitude of healings? By praying and seeing the definitive answers to those prayers? By going to church and seeing that people there are different?

Interestingly, no. My atheist friend said I can't use anecdotes to prove the existence of God. He meant stories I told about miracles I had witnessed. Those weren't enough. When I asked him if seeing a miracle would work, he said only if he saw ten or twelve himself. (Which, by the way, would still be considered anecdotal evidence!)

Although he sought signs, my other friend sought wisdom. He wanted a logical conclusion and a sound argument. Nothing has changed in what the world wants from God to believe in Him.

But God doesn't want us to believe in the things He does for us or the things He teaches us. Instead, He wants us to believe in Him. The evidence—the only evidence—He chooses to offer us is the cross.

Here's what I mean. It doesn't matter if anyone else is healed, Jesus is still the Christ. It doesn't matter if another prayer is answered, Jesus is still the Christ. The actions of the church don't determine the truth of the Gospel; Jesus is still the Christ.

Healing doesn't save. Answered prayer doesn't save. Christian behavior doesn't save.

Jesus saves.

IF ONLY THIS WERE TRUE IN THE CHURCH

This is a hard teaching, and different than what we often experience on Sunday mornings. I'm a preacher, so I know the pressure all those men and women who lead the churches are under. Every week, forty or fifty times a year, we get about half an hour to convince everyone to follow Jesus. We try every way we can dream up.

Topical sermons with application. Exegetical preaching, line by line through a book of the Bible. Reactive sermons based on current events in the church or the world. Proactive sermons that promote godliness and warn of temptation and sin.

That's a lot of pleading, teaching, cajoling, fire and brimstone, heaven and angels, grace, and truth. I can't tell you how disheartening it is to put so much work into such a small part of our ministry and see so little come from it. Is this too real? Maybe it is, and maybe I'll have editors cut this out later.

Just know I'm not frustrated here, not railing at church members. I'm lamenting because I think I've forgotten something important. Maybe other preachers have, too.

We don't need to convince our people of what God will do for them from now on. We need to convince them that what God did for them was enough.

Let's just say for a moment that it's true. Jesus came to earth, fully God and fully man. He was miraculously conceived and lived a sinless life. He taught the very Word of God and raised up the Twelve to continue after Him. He allowed Himself to be arrested, convicted, and crucified to fulfill God's plan of salvation for all of mankind.

Let's just say for a moment the benefits are real. We are made holy by His sacrifice. We are saved from hell, saved for heaven. We have eternal life waiting for us, a life that starts the moment we say yes to Him as Lord and Savior.

What more could we want? A better job? A gorgeous spouse? Obedient children? Money, prestige, power, fame?

I'm not saying it's wrong to ask for things. I'm saying it's wrong to say you won't believe in Him until He gives you something more. He's already given His life. Isn't that enough?

In the church, we find people who are waiting for God to give them more. Miracles that favor them. In the world, we find people who are waiting for God to give them more. Evidence that favors them.

God is waiting for people who are willing to put their faith in Him for what He's already done for us. This isn't a lifestyle that works better than all the others (although it is in the long run!), it is a call to follow a King worthy of following.

An allegiance, if you will.

BECOME: Saved for Transformation

As we explore each frustration, we are following the example of Jesus in His Sermon on the Mount. We need to Know the truth about Him so we can Be His and Live following His way. This volume is about the Gospel, but it directly addresses my frustration about faith and salvation. I have for most of my time as a believer struggled with this.

What does it mean to have faith? And if I learn that answer, how can I be assured of my salvation?

I remember sitting in a class about spiritual formation and someone asking how we know if we are saved. My professor smiled and said, "If you weren't saved, you wouldn't ask the question."

Think about it. The person who doesn't believe Jesus is the way isn't waking up every day wondering if Jesus has saved him. Only those who have come to understand certain truths about Jesus think to ask the question. If we believe He is the

Son of God, the Christ—that He died and rose again and belief in Him is the only way to reconciliation with the Father—then we need only reaffirm belief in those truths to answer our own question.

Up to this point, we've mostly dealt with my frustration about my faith. Even as we dealt with the Gospel of Jesus, we were tackling issues of faith more than issues of salvation. That's okay, though. Faith leads to salvation, and most of those conversations put us in a position to receive redemption.

We can now turn to salvation as we realize our faith (allegiance) opens the door. Not belief in a work, a sign, a wisdom, or an answered prayer. Not belief in a lifestyle or a culture. Not adherence to a Law or a collection of benefits.

Faith in (allegiance to) Jesus Christ is what leads us to eternal life.

Let me remind us of what frustrates me about my salvation by quoting from the first book, *Rethink*.

I was told that grace was a free gift, that I didn't need to earn anything. That God would transform me and that I would only need to believe in Him to have eternal life. But oh, by the way, you need to stop dressing like that and you can't talk that way and you can't dance, smoke OR chew, or go with girls that do.

I got a healthy dose of what I was saved from, but I wasn't told until after my commitment what I was saved for. Now, to be honest, the church where I was baptized was great at trying to share this with me. I admit this was

the attitude of the members of the church around me more
than the teaching of the leaders. Still, I was confused.
If grace is free, why do I need to change?

WHAT WE ARE SAVED FROM

I was asked once to give a one-sentence response to this question: "What does Jesus save us from?"

The person who asked would never be satisfied with the one-word answer my training had prompted in me: sin. Jesus saves us from sin. I thought about sin and remembered that we see two dynamics in the Bible's description, the sinful nature, and sinful acts: who we are as well as what we've done. These were church words, though, and I knew he would never be happy with a description using church words. I thought some more.

"Jesus saves me from the reality of who I am without Him."

I'd never really thought of it that way. Now I can't think of it any other way.

Here's the reality of who I am without God. My mom is a sweet lady who struggled to raise us through a divorce, through financial hardship, through dozens of moves, and lots of lost opportunities. She is a product of her own struggling childhood, but she worked to make something more of her children.

My dad is a free spirit who struggled to parent us through a divorce, through financial hardship, through dozens of moves, and some bad decisions. He is a product of his own struggling childhood, but he believed we could be as free as he was and yet make more of ourselves than he did.

They both screwed up countless times, and I am a product of those mistakes.

They both loved me as best they could, and I am a product of that love.

On my own, I found ways to screw up my own life. Education was a rare source of stability and I was smart enough to get through high school without much study and still be third in my class. Yet, I went to college four times before I could finish a degree.

I learned about girls and beer and whiskey and how to do bad things without getting caught. My friends were there to support me; sometimes, I was willing to support them. I didn't learn much about how to manage finances and it has hounded me most of my life.

I care about people, but I care just as deeply about what they think of me. I'm afraid of success but more afraid of failure. I'm prone to believe anything that will make me look good and prone to doubt anything that will expose me for who I really am.

I love doing the right thing, especially if it costs me something so that people will think I'm a great guy. I lie about doing the wrong thing because I don't want people to think I'm a bad guy. Mostly, I live for myself unless helping someone else gives me a good feeling or makes me look good.

I'm human.

Not everyone is like me. Some are better humans than me. Some are worse. Some are much worse. (My ego won't let me admit there might be some humans much better than me.) But the point is that I'm not perfect now, let alone before Jesus.

Maybe you're reading this and think I've run to religion because of a deep sense of shame. Not true. I like me, often liked me before I knew Jesus. Yet I always knew I had done things that were harmful to others and me. When I learned about Jesus in that first letter of John, it helped me to recognize these things as sins and taught me that they also caused a rift in my relationship with God.

In other words, I knew my shortcomings before I knew the word "sin." What I tried to do was make up for it. I'd try to do more good things than bad and outweigh the negative so that I could feel better. Really never worked, and no wonder. No matter what good I did, I was still guilty of my sins, my harmful acts, and my rift with God.

Notice I didn't say I felt guilty. I was guilty. Honestly, I *am* guilty as charged. Doing good things doesn't change that.

Imagine you rob a bank and take a million dollars. You go home and feel bad about it, but you know if you return the money you'll face the consequences. Can't fess up, but what about donating it? You look online and find this orphanage in a major city near you. They are about to close if they don't get help with funding.

Excited to cancel your crime, you go down to the orphanage and leave the million dollars in a bag at the front door. You ring the doorbell, dash across the street, and watch the secretary come to the door. He finds the bag, lights up, and scoops it into his arms. The director comes to see what's all the ruckus and she is surprised by a million-dollar anonymous donation. The orphanage is saved! You feel better (you kept a hundred thousand for yourself anyway), so you go home.

The police are there.

They have you on camera robbing the bank. They ask you to confess and to return the money. You smile. They'll forgive you once they know where most of the money is! You tell them the money has been given to save the orphanage downtown and you are willing to give your portion back to the bank. Aren't they glad you're such a good person?

Guess what? You're still going to jail. Despite your good deed, you still committed a crime. Also, the orphanage has to give all the money back, even if they spent some of it. Maybe you just hurried the closing of an important resource in the city.

In the same way, despite any good I have done in my life, I'm still guilty of the acts I chose to commit that hurt others, that hurt me, that caused a rift between me and God.

What's worse, that's *who I am* without God. I do that stuff all the time and I try to feel better about it. God used John's letter to put a spotlight on my character and myself. I suddenly realized the truth. I liked the darkness because of the darkness in me.

But there's hope.

For we ourselves were once foolish, disobedient, led astray, slaves to various passions and pleasures, passing our days in malice and envy, hated by others and hating one another.

— Titus 3:3

I love this passage because of the tone it takes when Paul talks about our sins. We were foolish, not evil. We were disobedient, not mean. We were led astray, not choosing the wrong path. We were slaves, not owners.

Sin doesn't mean I am evil. Sin means I am broken. I'm not a shameful person. I'm a guilty person.

I am not able to live in a way that benefits me and the people around me the most. Something always gets in the way, even if it's as sneaky as doing the right thing for someone just to feel better about myself. When Jesus gave the Sermon on the Mount, He upped the ante on righteousness. We couldn't just avoid the wrong thing, we had to avoid the heart that led us to do the wrong thing.

You have heard that it was said to those of old, "You shall not murder, and whoever murders will be liable to judgment." But I say to you that everyone who is angry with his brother will be liable to judgment…"

— Matthew 5:21-22a

When I'm broken, I can easily get frustrated with the people around me. That frustration can lead to anger, and anger can lead to murder. Jesus asked us not only to avoid murder but to avoid the heart that leads to murder. If I learn to handle my frustration, I need not worry about the rule that says murdering people is wrong.

But that also means it's a sin to let that frustration be the motivation for my actions.

That's the reality of who we are without Him. War, bullying, power trips, sexual misconduct, all of it comes down to who rules our hearts. And we are all guilty of letting our hearts and minds ponder our kind of justice for those who frustrate us.

God saves us from the reality of who we are by paying the debt for that guilt when Jesus came to earth, lived a perfect life, and died for you and me. The Gospel includes this, but it does not end here. Know why?

Because He loves you too much to leave you in this messy way of living life.

WHAT WE ARE SAVED FOR

Okay, Already Believers, I have you in mind as I continue. Not Yet Believers, keep listening. This is the part of the Gospel that we occasionally reference but rarely come out and say.

God is not interested in your reformation. He is interested in your transformation.

A butterfly lays eggs on a leaf and those eggs hatch. They are larvae and they spend their days eating the leaves and growing into caterpillars. Four or five times during the caterpillar's life, it sheds its skin. The caterpillar is reforming every so often, but it remains a caterpillar until it is fully grown and enters a cocoon. The time in the cocoon can last from a few weeks to two years. In that process, something is growing inside them, latent cells before are becoming legs and antennae and…wings!

Finally, the cocoon opens and the caterpillar has become what we know as a butterfly.

Two truths come from this. First, reformation did not turn the creature into a butterfly, transformation did. Second, *it was always a butterfly!* Remember who laid the eggs? A butterfly! From birth, the insect was always destined to be a butterfly. The only thing that can prevent it is death before the transformation.

In the same way, God always intended you to be an ultimate version of you—the holy you. The Gospel is the process of transformation. The only thing that can stop you from becoming the ultimate version of you is…death.

You are saved from the reality of who you are without Him because you were always destined to be who you are with Him. He is your King and has done all He can to earn your allegiance (faith) so that He can lead you to your best self.

I don't think a caterpillar ever existed that chose not to get in the cocoon, but we do this all the time. Why? Because you are not a robot, an automaton, not simply an animal. You are the pinnacle of God's creation, made in His image so that He might have fellowship with you.

You've learned this if you've heard the Gospel. God not only saves you from the reality of who you are without Him; He saves you for the reality of who you can be with Him.

71

God saves you for fellowship with Him.

That's a church word, so let me explain the fullness of what this means. I love this because it opened a door in me that I didn't expect. I mentioned before that I'm afraid of success but even more afraid of failure.

Fellowship with God means I don't need to be afraid of either.

Go to an American church today and ask about fellowship. Immediately, people will excitedly tell you that they love to have fellowship in their church. They'll talk about potlucks small groups and Sunday School classes. They'll tell you how friendly their members are on Sunday mornings and that they love spending time together.

In the Greek, the word is *koinonia*. Many churches today have a class or group that meets under this name. It's a feminine noun, Strong's concordance tells me, and it means to share something in common.

> *We proclaim to you what we have seen and heard, so that you also may have fellowship with us. And our fellowship is with the Father and with His Son, Jesus Christ.*
>
> *— 1 John 1:3*

John opens his letter with this thought. Jesus, Who is and was and is to come, was really human and those who knew Him can testify to it because they saw Him, touched Him, and lived life with Him. John wants us to know what he saw and heard so that we can "share in common" this knowledge about the Messiah. If we share that knowledge in common, in a way we also share this mystery with God and His Son Jesus.

We would be comfortable in a potluck sitting with John and Jesus because we share in common the knowledge of Who Jesus really is. Because of His promises, we can share even more in common.

> …He has granted to us His precious and very great promises, so that through them you may become partakers of the divine nature…
>
> — 2 Peter 1:4

Not only the mystery of the identity of Jesus, we also have in common the very divine nature of Jesus. We are in communion with Him. We know how to behave and we know who we can become.

But this passage uses *koinonos,* the masculine form of the Greek word for fellowship. That's why the English Standard Version uses the word "partakers" to designate it. This word implies more than the relationship of the first one. This isn't about potlucks or Sunday School classes. This form of the word fellowship means partnership, co-missionaries, sharing in common the work being done. To partake is to engage, to participate.

The relationship is important, and we are saved from sin so that we might have this kind of fellowship with God. But His "precious and very great promises" are not just for our relationship with Him. They invite us to "partake of the divine nature," to be godly, to act in godliness, and to love people the way God loves them. To do the work with God, be His partner.

This is the transformation faith (allegiance) brings to us, and it's for our good.

His resurrection saves me from myself. My yes to Him is for me first, but if it was only for me then He would immediately transport me to be with Him. Instead, He leaves me here just like He left Mack and my girlfriend's mom; because my yes is for the next person to see Jesus in me to encourage them to give Him their faith (allegiance).

I am transformed! A new creation with the purpose of becoming what God always intended me to be. It's not becoming a version of myself that I wouldn't want. No, the version of me God is bringing about is the best of me and what I would really want if I just believed it was even possible.

My environment can make that messy, but it can't overcome it.

My past mistakes can make people doubt me, but they can't define me anymore.

My idea of life—the work, the fun, the relationships—becomes clearer.

I am saved from sin for transformation so others can be saved for transformation.

I become completely His.

PART 3

LIVE

HEART: Reform or Transform?

I love God, love life, and know myself well. I recognize my weaknesses and admit to them up front as often as I can. Despite my desire to be faithful, I fail often. When I first became a believer, I would beat myself up for days when I willingly sinned. As I matured, I would profess my devotion to God, tell Him how sorry I was, and follow my confession with some version of "I know I gotta do better."

That's such a humbling statement, and I always felt better when I said it. In my heart, I was trying to model a willingness to be transparent and a desire to improve in my walk with Jesus. Many of us who follow Jesus feel this way even if we won't admit it.

"I gotta do better" is about reformation. When Martin Luther tacked his 95 theses on the door of Wittenberg, he wasn't denouncing the Catholic Church or trying to create a new church. He desired to reform the Catholic Church based on the issues he saw preventing her from acting as the Bride of Christ. That's why we call it The Reformation.

To reform is not to change something's nature. To reform something is to make changes that will improve it. This is a worthy cause.

All of us should want to get better. Sin less, obey more. Fall in line with the will of God and stop fighting Him for kingship in our lives. To reform is a worthy goal.

But it's not what God desires for us.

> *Therefore, if anyone is in Christ, he is a new creation. The old has passed away; behold the new has come.*
> — *2 Corinthians 5:17*

This passage doesn't speak of reformation. Our hearts are too sick for that. When we frame our faith journey with, "I gotta do better," we unwittingly trade in the great and settle for the good. It is good to want to reform. But we are not reformed versions of ourselves in the Good News.

We are brand new. Transformed.

In our desire to please God, we have accidentally set ourselves up for failure. Those of us who Already Believe know we are sinners until the day we die. We just hope we can reform ourselves a little bit at a time so that people will see our efforts and think maybe this Christian thing could work for them, too.

So we focus on ourselves. We go to church to learn how to be better, go to classes to learn more Bible to be better, and go to small groups to live life with other Christians to be better. All of our efforts seem to bring about only marginal change, though.

Why?

Because God is not interested in our reformation.

The caterpillar that goes into the cocoon doesn't come out a better caterpillar. She comes out as a butterfly. Her transformation is complete. She never really was a caterpillar and will never be a caterpillar again.

God has done the same thing in our hearts if we put our faith (allegiance) in Him. Paul tries to explain it to us in Romans using the idea of resurrection. Fitting, isn't it, since our Lord saved us through His?

> *For if we have been united with Him in a death like His, we shall certainly be united with Him in a resurrection like His. We know that our old self was crucified with Him in order that the body of sin might be brought to nothing, so that we would no longer be enslaved to sin.*
> — *Romans 6:5-6*

Don't know about you, but I struggle with this passage. My old self still likes to be alive. That's how it feels, anyway. Much of my Christian walk has been riddled with failure and becoming a pastor didn't automatically change that. Some days I didn't think of God at all until I messed up. Then I couldn't think of anything else.

No wonder we are thought of as sticks in the mud. Every time we start to do something the world thinks is fun, we beat ourselves up about it. Sometimes, we beat up everyone around us about it, too.

Complete honesty here. Sometimes it helps me to rant about someone else's sin. Why is that? It doesn't really make me a better person. Certainly doesn't make me look better. Why am I so quick to judge others for making the mistakes I make?

Because I've bought into the lie that I need reformation and therefore an excuse for when I'm not reformed. That others are missing the mark makes me feel like I'm not the only one. But listen, reformation will never transform me. No, the truth is that God has already transformed me.

A LAZARUS OR JESUS RESURRECTION?

One of my favorite stories is only in John. Jesus has some friends, a brother and two sisters, and while He is away the brother takes sick. The sisters know Jesus is the Messiah, so they send for Him. Jesus waits. Two days.

When He arrives, He learns Lazarus died four days ago (John 11:39). Twice, Jesus is "deeply moved" and weeps as He considers His friend's death. The humanity of this is evident but think of the divinity of it. God never wanted this for His children. Eternal life was always His plan for them. No wonder He wept.

From the very beginning, He tells the sister named Martha that Lazarus will rise again. Yet when Jesus tells them to roll the stone away from the tomb, Martha complains that the body will stink after so long. She said she believed He was the Christ (11:27) but she can't believe He can manage this.

Jesus said to her, "Did I not tell you that if you believed you would see the glory of God?
— *John 11:40*

They roll it away and Jesus tells Lazarus to come out. Imagine the risk He is taking here. After all He has done—including raising others from the dead—never has He done this with someone who is four days dead. If this doesn't work, His credibility takes a hit.

Yet He does because He knows the power He has. No miracle is too big for the One Who created the world, created mankind, created Lazarus. The King has no doubts about Himself. Martha may believe and yet doubt, but Jesus has no doubt what is about to happen.

When He had said these things, He cried out with a loud voice, "Lazarus, come out." The man who had died came out, his hands and feet bound with linen strips, and his face wrapped with a cloth. Jesus said to them, "Unbind him, and let him go."
— *John 11:43-44*

Don't miss this. Lazarus is resurrected and when he comes out, he is still wearing his grave clothes. Jesus has to tell someone to take them off of him.

That's completely different from the resurrection that happens later in John. This time it's only three days, but there's no Messiah outside the tomb to raise Jesus. No, the Messiah is inside the tomb and Mary Magdalene is distraught that the stone is rolled away and the body is gone. Peter and John rush to the tomb to find out if this is true. John gets there first, but he's afraid to go in.

> *Then Simon Peter came, following him, and went into the tomb. He saw the linen cloths lying there, and the face cloth, which had been on Jesus' head, not lying with the linen cloths but folded up in a place all by itself.*
>
> — *John 20:6-7*

This is a different resurrection, isn't it? The Messiah was not outside the tomb, but inside. The graveclothes were not still on Him, they were folded neatly and left in the tomb. The same Messiah performed both miracles, but the second one is greater. Later, when they see Jesus, He's dressed like a gardener (20:14).

Which resurrection is Jesus offering us?

> *For if we have been united with Him in a death like His, we shall certainly be united with Him in a resurrection like His. We know that our old self was crucified with Him in order that the body of sin might be brought to nothing . . .*
>
> — *Romans 6:5-6a*

THE WALKING DEAD

I know, cheap subtitle. But it sets me up to ask this question: why are so many Christians walking around in grave clothes?

Interestingly, our graveclothes are different than they were back in Jesus' day. They wore something ceremonial yet practical, but what do we wear? Our Sunday best! Suits mostly, dresses, favorite outfits. We want our corpses to "look their best" or to represent who we were. I even heard of a grandmother who asked for an M&M® Candy-themed casket and had herself dressed for the occasion.

At some point, we decided the ceremonial robes weren't enough. We wanted the person to look like they were still alive and experiencing their best day, or like they were still alive and enjoying their favorite part of their former lives. Sometimes, we do the same to ourselves in our spiritual lives. Instead of embracing the new life we are given, we dress up the old one so that it looks better.

God doesn't want to dress us in better graveclothes, though. He wants us to fold up our graveclothes neatly and walk out of the tomb naked!

Wait. Maybe I went too far. But seriously, we leave the tomb the same way we left the womb—completely new and vulnerable. Like we were before we could make our own decisions, we are babies who will have to learn how to live life. At first, we need lots of nutrition that we can't get ourselves. Our spiritual parents may have to help us learn how to sit up, crawl, walk, and run.

Too many of us, though, act like we are the old us and clutch our Sunday best around us. We're so glad we've been resurrected, but we live in the new life of Lazarus instead of the new life of Christ.

You were made for more than that.

You were made for holiness from the very beginning. Not pie-in-the-sky, goody-two-shoes, no-fun-having you. Set apart you. New you.

Planted in the middle of a zombie apocalypse. Unlike the poor saps in *The Walking Dead*, though, you know the root of the sickness that caused it and you have the cure, for you and the person in front of you.

To live this, you have to believe this in your heart. The matter is settled. Done. No one can take this from you. You are the new you if you give your faith (allegiance) to Jesus on the evidence that He died and rose again to free you from the grave.

Take those things off. Put on these new clothes, brother, sister…

> *Put on then, as God's chosen ones, holy and beloved, compassionate hearts, kindness, humility, meekness, and patience, bearing with one another and, if one has a complaint against another, forgiving each other; as the Lord has forgiven you, so you also must forgive.*
> — *Colossians 3:12-13*

…and be transformed.

The world will tell you it isn't enough. They will want you to join them in what they think is fun. But once you start realizing Jesus saved you from the reality of who you are without Him, you will let Him transform you into who you are with Him.

The real you.

But you have to put your faith in (give your allegiance to) the One who saved you to see it. And that's not "believing without evidence." It's seeing the truth of who Jesus is and what He offers you.

After all, you were always meant to be that butterfly.

SOUL: Spirit Power vs. Will Power

The reason reformation doesn't work is because our nature is as wrong as our actions. We are selfish people, not just people who do selfish things. I wish that wasn't true, but I can prove it. Do me a favor and go to a local bookstore.

First, look for the "self-help" section. Now, look for the "help-others" section.

When you've covered the whole bookstore without finding the second section, go back to the first section and look for the number of "self-help" books that indicated by the title that the best way to help yourself is to help others.

Even when we want to become better people, we start by being selfish.

Someone will no doubt remind me of the airplane analogy. The flight attendant always tells us to put our own oxygen masks on first before we try to help others. You make a valid point. I'm not arguing against it, exactly; I'm just pointing out our nature. Without God, we look to ourselves first, second, third, thousandth, and then to others.

The oxygen mask is your salvation, not your sanctification. Once you are saved (put on your oxygen), you should start getting masks for everyone else. Believing God wants you to become a better person before you share the Gospel with others is like believing you should tidy up your area, put on fresh clothes, and get your luggage out of the overhead bin before putting oxygen masks on the people around you.

Look to yourself first, yes. But don't gaze at your navel for years after.

Sadly, we are often just as selfish with what we are learning about God after we are saved. This is why so many of us get trapped into a pattern of Christian self-help and wear our graveclothes to the Feast of Heaven. Every day, we gussy up for God and try to do better. Some wills are stronger than others, but all wills fall short of the glory of God.

Falling short of the glory of God. This is another Scripture reference we Christians like to abuse. We quote it to defend our human frailty ("To err is human...") and make ourselves feel better as we work on reform. But Paul uses this phrase to talk about transformation, not reformation. Look at the context of this popular phrase. This is another long passage I encourage you not to pass over. See it with new eyes:

> *But now the righteousness of God has been manifested apart from the law, although the Law and the Prophets bear witness to it—the righteousness of God through faith*

in Jesus Christ for all who believe. For there is no distinction: for all have sinned and fall short of the glory of God, and are justified by His grace as a gift, through the redemption that is in Christ Jesus...

— Romans 3:21-24

When we quote this passage, we often think of our own righteousness (or, most often, the lack thereof). But this passage speaks to the righteousness of God. We don't "get better" by believing in Jesus. We are freed from our righteousness to take on the righteousness of God!

It couldn't happen under the Law because all the Law could do is show us how far short we come on our own. The Law shows us the reality of who we are without God. It is good, fair, and right, but it is unable to make us obey or help us attain the righteousness it asks from us.

That's why a Truth-only Gospel can be dangerous. We end up feeling ashamed of ourselves most of the time as we fail time and again. This is not freedom, brothers and sisters. God didn't save us to bring us back under judgment.

Instead, the righteousness of God, not our own, is available to us if we give our faith (allegiance) to Jesus. The Law and the Prophets bear witness to it, but they can't deliver it. Only Jesus can deliver it. This isn't a reason to feel better about sinning sometimes. This is a gateway to freedom from who we were without God to the reality of who we are with God.

So stop willing yourself to be better. Start trusting Jesus that He has made you whole.

Gives a whole new meaning to "let go and let God," doesn't it? But don't we still sin? Yes, sadly, we still sin sometimes. We have rough patches, make poor decisions, react poorly to the decisions of others, and forget or ignore God. Then don't we have to try to get better? What other way is there?

The Way. First, we have to understand what God means when He inspired the writers of the New Testament to tell us to have "self-control."

A REFRESHER ON THE SOUL

Not Yets may have skipped the first volume to read this, and some Alreadys didn't know about the first one when they picked this up. I want to teach or reteach first the difference between soul and spirit.

> (For those armchair theologians who believe we are binary, not trinary—that we have bodies but that "soul" and "spirit" are the same thing—bear with me. Think of it in the same way Jesus added to the Great Commandment to help the people understand in their Greek culture that "soul" and "mind" are two halves of a whole but just separate enough to require them both for explanation.)

The prophet Isaiah is telling Israel how God can be trusted to provide for them and to treat them with lovingkindness.

In the middle of it, he writes an ode to God that describes his response to God. In the middle of *that*, he writes:

> *My soul yearns for you in the night; my spirit within me earnestly seeks you.*
>
> — *Isaiah 26:9*

The first word he uses to describe himself is *nephesh*, the Hebrew word translated as soul. Strong's concordance defines this as many things, but all point to the self, the identity of the person, and who the person is. What does this person's soul do in the passage? He yearns, craves, greatly desires. He's in bed, late at night, and the identity of that person longs for God.

The second word is *ruach*, which is translated as spirit. This is not the same word, nor does it have the same meaning. Strong's concordance defines it as breath, wind, and spirit. What does this person's spirit in the passage do? He earnestly seeks, he is diligently after God. His spirit is not craving God as something to be possessed, he is on a mission to find God. *Ruach* is the word often used for the Holy Spirit.

Paul makes the same distinction in his letter to the Thessalonians.

> *Now may the God of peace Himself sanctify you completely, and may your whole spirit and soul and body be kept blameless at the coming of our Lord Jesus Christ.*
>
> — *1 Thessalonians 5:23*

Here the two words are *pneuma* for spirit, used of the Holy Spirit, and *psyche* for soul. Again, the word for spirit can also mean breath or wind. The parallel is exact. And the *psyche*? It means distinct identity, will, and the seat of affection.

In other words, in both testaments, a distinction is made between our identity, who we are, and some other part of us that is also us but at least in words is attached to the Holy Spirit. We are split in two inside our flesh.

A quick word about the flesh—this is what the old-timers called our "carnal desires," the animal instincts that drive many of our decisions in the reality of who we are without God. The *psyche* that fights against those desires for the greater good of mankind is what elevates us above other animals. It gives even those who do not believe in God the ability to choose a higher road instead of taking advantage of those around us. The *pneuma* that diligently seeks God, however, is what moves us to satisfaction when we act selflessly and guilt if we are too selfish too often. The *pneuma* proves we are made in His image and can be something even greater.

Follow this. If we were left to our flesh, we would always be selfish to the point of evil. Because of our souls, we yearn to benefit the community even if it means being selfless, thus avoiding evil. Because of our spirits, when we are selfless we realize the higher good we have served; when we are selfish and harm ourselves and others, we realize what we have done is evil and that we've broken our relationship with God and feel guilty for it.

This is why Paul says,

I appeal to you therefore, brothers, by the mercies of God, to present your bodies (flesh) *as a living sacrifice, holy and acceptable to God, which is your spiritual worship. Do not be conformed to this world, but be transformed by the renewing of your mind* (psyche)*, that by testing you may discern what is the will of God, what is good and acceptable and perfect.*

— *Romans 12:1-2* (parentheses mine)

Isaiah wrote before the resurrection of Christ when the Holy Spirit had not yet been given to all mankind. His reference is the Law and the desire to follow the Law. It's up to him in his spirit to diligently seek God and in his soul to crave God above all else. He has to rely on his *nephesh* to control his actions while his *ruach* seeks the *Ruach Hakkodesh*, The Holy Spirit.

For us, though, Paul is writing after the resurrection, when Peter quotes the prophet Joel to tell us the Holy Spirit has been poured out on all of us:

And in the last days it shall be, God declares, that I will pour out my Spirit (Pneuma)*, on all flesh, and your sons and your daughters shall prophesy…*

— *Acts 2:17a,* (parenthesis mine)

How does this make us different? Isaiah continues by talking about how the world "learns righteousness" (Isaiah 26:9b) through God's judgments. In other words, we like David should fall in love with His statutes and ordinances because in them we learn how to be more righteous. Isaiah is basically saying, "God, I really crave You and a part of me seeks You diligently. I know by how You judge things that You are righteous and I want to be like that, too. Help me be better, because I gotta do better."

But Paul finishes his thought a different way. Look at the passage in Thessalonians again:

> *Now may the God of peace Himself sanctify you completely, and may your whole spirit and soul and body be kept blameless at the coming of our Lord Jesus Christ. He who calls you is faithful; He will surely do it.*
> — *1 Thessalonians 5:23-24*

Do you see it? God is the One who sanctifies you and because He is faithful, He will surely do it! This is not your own effort—it's His! Sanctification is His work on you, not your work for Him.

The soul in us—the identity, who we are, the seat of our affections and will—can crave God all it wants, but it can't get us to God. But the spirit in us—breath, wind—resonates with the Holy Spirit and seeks God diligently. Jesus, then, provides for us the righteousness we can't attain on our own.

So, then, why does the Bible talk about self-control?

HOLDING YOUR WATER

No denying it, on the list of the fruit of the Spirit in Galatians 5:22-23 is something called "self-control." The Greek word means to hold mastery or dominion over oneself, to restrain ourselves from something we want to do and can reference continence.

Yeah, that's right. It means to "hold your water" when you really have to go to the bathroom. Great at visual images, the Greeks. Self-control means bobbing up and down because you know it isn't right to wet your pants. Doesn't this illustrate what it feels like sometimes to reform?

We hold off as long as we can, wondering if we can wait long enough to let the feeling pass. Sometimes, even as we hold it in, we know it's just a matter of time before it comes anyway.

When I try to master my desires, it often feels this way to me. I'm saying no—and part of me is proud of myself for it—but underneath I know my soul is losing the battle. I've put it off, but I haven't defeated it.

I think that's why Peter puts it so far down the list when he describes what a mature believer looks like. You know that list? Let me show you.

...make every effort to supplement your faith with virtue, and your virtue with knowledge, and knowledge with self-control...

— 2 Peter 1:5-6a

Faith comes first because, without allegiance to Christ, it is impossible. That faith, then, leads to virtue—understanding what is right—which leads to the knowledge we need to strengthen our faith. Only after that comes self-control.

Yet, when someone seeks Jesus, what do we do in the church? We walk them through a plan of salvation, most likely get them baptized, and then tell them they now must have self-control. We'll help, though, by providing knowledge so that they can be more virtuous.

We got it backward, folks, because we forgot the list in Galatians is the fruit of the Spirit, not the root of the Spirit.

Fruit is not something that produces something; no, fruit is what is produced. Now, true, the fruit has seeds in it to make more of its kind (which came first, the chicken or the egg?). But the concept Paul is trying to teach us is that the Spirit within us speaks to our spirit, *Pneuma* to *pneuma*, and the fruit of that is, among other things, being able to hold our water.

Look at how he starts the passage that contains the fruit of the Spirit:

> *But I say, walk by the Spirit, and you will not gratify the desires of the flesh. For the desires of the flesh are against the Spirit, and the desires of the Spirit are against the flesh, for these are opposed to each other, to keep you from doing the things you want to do.*
>
> — *Galatians 5:16-18*

I'll have much more to say about walking in the Spirit in the last volume of this series. For now, recognize this truth: God through the resurrection of Jesus Christ opened the door for the Spirit to dwell *in* you, not with you. The power you have inside you can overcome the desires that cause you to hurt yourself, hurt others, and break your relationship with God. All we need to do is recognize the gift for what it is. We won't be sinless, but we also won't be fruitlessly trying to do better. Our identity will be in Christ, not in our goodness.

You are not ever going to be a better Christian by yourself; and that's not the point, anyway. One more passage to back this up before we talk about what it means for us. In fact, it frames the "so what?" of this conversation.

> *...for God gave us a Spirit, not of fear, but of power and love and self-control.*
>
> — *2 Timothy 1:7*

Many of the English versions of this letter use a lowercase *s* in this passage, but I once heard Gordon Fee comment at a conference that we should capitalize every reference of "spirit" in the New Testament unless the context convinces us otherwise. (A theology conference was held at Wheaton in Chicago, Illinois, in the spring of 2011 where I got to see him and Dallas Willard discuss discipleship.) I agree with him, especially in this passage.

Our own spirits do not give us power and love and self-control.

The Spirit gives us power and love and self-control.

RECAP FOR OUR NOT YETS FIRST

I remember sitting in a Methodist Church at the age of seventeen beside my (different) girlfriend and her mother. The minister preached the Gospel that day, but I had no frame of reference. He mentioned the evil sin of abortion without knowing I had only the year before got a previous girlfriend pregnant and paid for the abortion.

I wasn't convicted of my sin. I was angry at my girlfriend. I figured for him to preach that on just the Sunday I happened to be in the audience, she must have told him. I didn't want to repent of my sin (even though my heart ached at the thought of us killing my child). I wanted to start in on the minister to work up a sweat so I could really give it to my girlfriend.

That was the last time I went to a church until I tried to impress another girlfriend's mother and stumbled into Southeast Christian Church in Louisville, Kentucky.

Why? Because I didn't understand what he was offering. I got lost in his description of sin so I never got around to hearing his prescription for sin.

Not Yets, I don't want the same thing to happen to you. So here is a recap for those who have been lost in the weeds, as we used to say in the food service business.

- John the Baptist came to reveal to us the reality of who we are without God.
- He then asked us to believe that God wants us to discover the reality of who we are with Him. All we have

to do is rethink (repent of) our lives without Him and admit we have hurt ourselves, hurt others, and broken our relationship with Him.

- But he says Someone's coming who can mend that relationship completely for us.
- Jesus is that Someone, and He comes talking about the Kingdom of Heaven being available to us if we would do as John said: repent (rethink) and believe in Him.
- Living a life without hurting Himself and others while in complete connection with God, Jesus demonstrates His love for us by dying horribly on the cross for us.
- Proving His divinity, Jesus rises from the grave and puts on new clothes, leaving His graveclothes behind. He tells us He did this for us to pay the penalty for all our bad decisions, hurtful words, thoughtless actions, and selfishness. If we believe in His sacrifice for us, God will forgive us completely and bring about in us the reality of who we are with God.
- We experience the benefits of this willingness to put our faith in (give allegiance to) Jesus, but we also have responsibilities. No longer are we to be mastered by the kingdom of this world. We are now citizens of heaven under the rule and authority of Jesus. But that's good since what Jesus wants for all His citizens is to see the reality of who they were always meant to be.

- The greatest of those benefits is being filled today with the Holy Spirit. God wants something better for us than we can achieve on our own, so He gave us a Spirit of power, love, and self-control to help us live the life we never dreamed was possible.
- *Good News! The Kingdom of Heaven is reclaiming earth through the life, death, and resurrection of Jesus Christ of Nazareth, God's only Son. We who repent of our sins and give allegiance to Him are forgiven and empowered by the Holy Spirit to spread His influence as we boldly follow in His footsteps.*

The key to experiencing a new life is not to believe in Jesus and hope to do better. No, the key to new life is the Spirit of God, made available to you by God when you believe in His Son, Jesus. He is not only the prescription for forgiveness for all you've done; He's the antidote to all the wrong parts of you that make you do those things in the first place.

The Truth-only crowd wants you to stop sinning and do better.

The Grace-only crowd wants you to stop worrying about sinning and you'll do better.

The Grace-and-Truth Gospel wants you to realize God forgave your sinful acts *and* transformed the nature inside you that causes you to sin. All you have to do is believe Him. Put your faith in Him. Give your allegiance to Him.

How do we know when God has accomplished this in us?

POWER, LOVE, AND SELF-CONTROL

One of my favorite memories of my youngest son has to do with his disobedience. Well, not exactly. I'm sure I was upset at whatever he wasn't doing. What I love about the memory is how he responded when I told him to do what he was supposed to do. He looked me right in the eye and his little brow furrowed and he shouted with all his might, "I can't want it!"

Yeah. I feel that sometimes.

I don't know about you, but I struggle to give anyone else power over me. Despite all my talk of allegiance to (faith in) God, what I really want is to be the big man in charge. To be honest, when I can do it on my own, I feel great about it. Look at me, God! I'm doing it!

Then God says, "I know, and I told you to stop it."

I respond by furrowing my brow, looking Him right in the eye, and shouting, "I can't want it!"

Not that I don't want it, but I can't. Without the Spirit, this is exactly true. We *can't* want what He has for us because we don't even understand what it is. What we know is what we see and hear and feel and taste and smell. When God directs us beyond that, we don't trust what's beyond those senses unless it "makes sense" to us. We can't want it.

But the Power Paul tells Timothy he has isn't some greater ability to want what God has. No, that Power is the Spirit's, not his. If I can do it in my power, I can control it. God often moves us beyond our own power so that the illusion of control falls apart. The truth is, we are often either led by our animal instincts or our personal preferences.

God calls us to a life higher than that and then gives us the Power to accomplish it. What kind of life is He calling us to receive? A life of love. Real love. Love that transcends what we can give on our own. *Agape* love—unconditional, divine love.

We haven't talked much about the enemy that tries to keep us away from God. I think sometimes we give him power just by mentioning him, so I don't plan to go too deeply into the enemy's camp here. Let me just expose one way he has done a number on our society.

I love my wife. I love sex. I love my sisters. I love pizza.

If I'm talking to someone who understands English, they will naturally interpret what I mean by love in each of these examples. I imagine those four sentences could create confusion in someone who is just learning the language, though. Of course, I don't love pizza the same way I love my wife. But the grammar of the sentence doesn't tell someone that. The context of the noun following the verb "love" tells them.

In the Greek, this isn't the case. They use four different words for love and sometimes even combine two of them to mean something else. Let me define each.

- *Storge* is the word that means love of family. It's the "blood is thicker than water" love. If you've ever heard someone say, "I know how he is, but he's my brother," then you've experienced *storge* in someone.

- *Eros* is the word that means intimate, romantic love. It's where we get the word "erotic" and in Greek it is only slightly higher than *storge*. Typically, this kind of love is as much about what we get from the other person as what we give.

- *Philos* is what the Greeks thought was the highest form of human love. It's how deep friendship is described, brotherhood or sisterhood or community. A community that experiences this in such a way that they become family experiences *philostorge*, which is what Paul uses in Romans 12:10 when he says to "love one another with brotherly affection."

- *Agape* is the word for godly love, unconditional love, the ultimate love of all. This is the love that is to govern those of us who believe in Jesus, and this is the love Paul tells Timothy the Spirit gives us when he lists, "power, love, and self-control."

Why is this important to know?

Because that enemy's trick I talked about earlier was to supplant *agape* with *eros* as the highest love. When we think of love, we most often think of romantic love as the highest love we can attain. But all human loves – family, romance, friendship – were meant to be guided by godly love. Too often, we let all the other loves become guided by romantic love (enter Freud).

The great love story of our lives is the love of the Creator, not the love of another person. Why? Because only the Creator has perfect *agape* love for us and only the Creator can teach us to have *agape* love for Himself and other people.

But we can't want it without Him. Instead, we will substitute one of the human loves and interpret life through it. This is why people who don't believe in the Bible try to use it to trap us into their way of thinking. If God is love, why can't I sleep with who I want? Why can't I have as many partners as I want? Why can't you just let me have my love story since God is love?

Because God is *agape*, not *eros*.

And godly love will always align with God's version of our best life. To experience the best that human love has to offer, we have to let godly love control it. But we can't want it. Not without having the Power of the Spirit inside us for it.

What does all this have to do with self-control? Everything.

Follow the line of thinking Paul gives us. The Power comes from the Spirit, not from us, so it is perfect. The Love the Spirit shows us is godly love, not human love, so it is perfect. If we operate in the Power and the Love of the Spirit, we will have no trouble holding our water because it will be what is best for God, for us, and them.

God is not trying to reform our will so that we can be better. He is transforming our Power and Love so we can be the very best version of ourselves.

The reality of who we are with Him.

MIND: Deciding to Follow

When I was younger, I would take a trip every year to see a group of guys I knew in college. Most of them were serving God full-time. We had a Presbyterian, a Charismatic, a Latter Day Saint, a Christian Church, and a Church of Christ minister. Add to that an atheist, an agnostic, and some who were spiritually indifferent.

The campfire conversations were intense.

I relished those talks. We did other stuff because we are guys. All of us played Dungeons & Dragons in college, so we spent a day in a campaign. We saw Braveheart in the theater together once and left the building unable to talk yet about what we had shared. Part of the day was spent with homemade kendo swords beating on each other.

Guys, you know?

But what I miss the most are the conversations. One year we were moved to confession and shared our darkest parts of ourselves. Most years, though, we wrestled with our understanding of God and learned from each other's backgrounds.

Someone would share what they believed and I would nod my head because I liked what they had said so far. And then I would say...

"I agree with you, but . . ." and then share my more highly enlightened version of whatever they were talking about. In my mind, I wasn't offering a counterpoint. I was enlarging what had already been said. I agreed with them as far as their path had taken them. My hope was to help them take the next step down the path.

Humbly, of course.

Until one day I started out, "I agree with you, but..."

And one of my best friends said, "You know when you start that way we know it means you don't really agree."

I thought about it and realized he was right. If I really agreed with them, I would be able to stop there. "I agree with you." Maybe it was a way to let the person down softly. *Yes, yes, my friend, you are on the path. If only you were as wise as I am, you would take this next step and find out you really didn't have the whole picture.*

I agree with you meant I can condescend to their level, *but . . .* meant that I couldn't really condescend to their level because I knew better. Truly, I was disagreeing, not agreeing.

We tend to do the same with God.

God, You say we all have faults and errors and make poor decisions. You say that is sin and that it hurts others, hurts me, and breaks my relationship with You. I agree with You, but that's just how humans are. You shouldn't judge me for that.

God, You say we are guilty of the things we have done and that there is a penalty for our disobedience. I agree with You, but I've been doing a lot of good things, too. Don't I get any credit for that?

God, You say the penalty for my guilt is death, because my faults and errors and poor decisions brought about so much death in me, in others, and in my relationship with You. I agree with You, but a loving God shouldn't be so quick to condemn people and send them to hell.

God, You say You don't send people to hell but only provide the consequences of their actions—in effect, they send themselves to hell. I agree with You, but doesn't everybody deserve a second, third, fourth, millionth chance? Aren't You a forgiving God?

God, You say You sent Your son to live, die, and rise again to save me from the consequences of my sin. I agree with You, but if He ever really lived could He really rise from the grave? Isn't that against science?

God, You say all I need to do is believe in Your son to have eternal life; that He is the way, the truth, and the life, and that no one can come to You except through Him. I agree with You, but what about all the people worshiping in other religions? Don't they get a chance to go to heaven?

God, You say Your grace is sufficient for me. I agree with You, but what about the changes people expect me to make? How can grace be free if I have to think, speak, decide, act, and live differently?

God, You say all things work for the good of those who love You and are called according to Your purpose. I agree with You, but there's a lot of evil in the world and I still suffer sometimes. Can't you do something about that?

God, You say if I seek first Your kingdom and its righteousness then You will add all the things I worry about to my life. I agree with You, but I've been baptized, go to church three times a week, serve You faithfully, and forgive all the terrible people in my life; yet I still don't have all the things I want. What gives? (Or, more to the point, what *doesn't* give...)

God, You say that if enough of us follow Your Son it will bring change for the better to the whole world. I agree with You, but can't You just do it all by Yourself? You have the power, after all.

SANTA JESUS, KING JESUS

The truth is, when we say those things what we really mean is that we don't agree at all. If sin has caused me to face the death penalty and Jesus died to pardon me from that sentence—if He literally saved my eternal life—then why is life so hard? Why can't I be who I want to be? Why can't I just go back to the way things were before I met Him?

Even better, why can't He just make my life extraordinary? Take away all my suffering? Answer all my prayers? Heal all my sicknesses and injuries? Keep everyone I love from dying? Bless my socks off and expect nothing in return?

Maybe right here you're expecting me to blast you for thinking these things. Who said I was sharing your thoughts? I wish I knew you well enough to list what you are thinking because it might sell a whole lot more books. But these are my thoughts.

This is me. I want Santa Jesus, and not just because I'm selfish. I want him because I see Santa Jesus in the Bible.

Blessed are the poor in spirit, for theirs is the kingdom of heaven.

Blessed are those who mourn, for they shall be comforted.

Blessed are the meek, for they shall inherit the earth.

Blessed are those who hunger and thirst for righteousness, for they shall be satisfied.

Blessed are the merciful, for they shall receive mercy.

Blessed are the pure in heart, for they shall see God.

Blessed are the peacemakers, for they shall be called sons of God.

— *Matthew 5:3-8*

But seek first the kingdom of God and His righteousness, and all these things will be added to you.

— *Matthew 6:33*

Ask, and it will be given to you; seek, and you will find; knock, and the door will be opened to you.

— *Matthew 7:7*

They shall hunger no more, neither thirst anymore; the sun shall not strike them, nor any scorching heat, for the Lamb in the midst of the throne will be their shepherd, and He will guide them to springs of living water, and God will wipe away every tear from their eyes.
— Revelation 7:16-17

Maybe I just committed a mild form of blasphemy just coming up with the name Santa Jesus, let alone list places where Jesus offers us so many cool gifts. I don't think so, though. I'm not saying Santa Jesus is real. I'm saying Jesus is a giver.

Whether or not Jesus sometimes acts like Santa in His generosity isn't the issue. The real issue is that we often stop at this part of Him when we approach Him. He is a giver of many promises that sound good to us. We want those. He has promised to answer prayers for us. We want that. If we're really good this year, can we have them?

But King Jesus promised them, not Santa Jesus. He is granting, bestowing, and giving to us these precious and very great promises based on our understanding of who He really is and our willingness to acknowledge Him for it (2 Peter 1:3-4). When we recognize the King Who calls us to His own glory and excellence, we find ourselves falling at His feet, not shaking our fists and pointing to the empty space under the tree.

As our knees hit the floor, however, He allows our worship and then grabs us by the shoulders to pull us into a warm embrace. Our allegiance to (faith in) Him opens the door to the gifts. He is blessing His servant, not spoiling His offspring.

110

THE WRONG QUESTION

And yet, suffering still happens. Poor choices still bring consequences. Mean, spiteful people are still mean and spiteful to us. The worst of sins—murder, rape, violence—still happen after Jesus rose from the grave, even to the Twelve who were entrusted with His message.

How can these things be true and yet allow room in my understanding of God to explain all the bad things that happen? Even as a believer, I've lost loved ones, lost status and reputation through the actions of others, experienced sickness and injury. I've gone without and I've suffered emotional pain. Not all of my prayers have been answered. I've served Jesus and still been lied about, pushed aside, and marginalized.

What gives? How can I owe my allegiance to (put faith in) someone who seems to miss the mark on the things He promises? The question that most often wraps up this position of doubt is, "Why do so many bad things happen to good people?"

We could corner the market, Jesus, if You would just promise to alleviate all the heartache, doubt, and dilemma in the lives of Your faithful! Imagine how many people would want to follow You if they received everything they wanted as soon as they swore allegiance to (put faith in) You! Maybe God got this thing all wrong. If bad things never happened to the believers, it would be so much easier to believe!

God, You say that You know better how to run the world. I agree with You, but...

Maybe this is the reason some of my Not Yet believers have waited this long. They've heard all the arguments for how good God is and how Jesus plays a part. They've heard how the Spirit transforms us and how we can go to heaven. Maybe they've even heard that the benefits start way before we are granted admission to the "pearly gates." But they haven't heard an answer to that one question.

"Why do bad things still happen to believers? Why do they happen to good people?"

Great question. It's just the wrong question.

How we frame this shows a little bit of our view of the world. In the book of John, Jesus over and over tries to raise people's perspective above the earthly to the heavenly.

Nicodemus is confronted with the idea of being born again and he wonders how a grown man can re-enter his mother's womb. Jesus elevates his perspective by saying he must be born of water *and* the Spirit (John 3:5).

The woman at the well wants to know if the Samaritans or the Jews are the true worshipers. Jesus elevates her perspective to see that "…the hour is coming when neither on this mountain nor in Jerusalem will you worship the Father" (John 4:21). Instead *how* they worship will be more important than *where* (John 4:23).

The Jews want to know if Jesus is greater than those who gave them manna in the wilderness to sustain them. Jesus elevates their perspective with the revelation that He is the bread of life (6:41).

Here, we have to ask Jesus to do the same.

The question, "Why do bad things happen to good people?" supposes that God is the perpetrator of all that happens on the earth. If a bad thing happens, because God could prevent it we see Him as being responsible for it. Saying it out loud, reading it in a book, this seems ludicrous. But that's the perspective behind the question. The good that people do is because we have good people doing it. But if bad things happen, especially to good people, God is responsible.

Let me suggest the opposite question is the better one. Why do good things happen to bad people? Maybe even better, why do good things happen at all?

Barring natural disasters, nearly every bad thing that happens is caused by a decision of another human being. We know this is true when it comes to the vicious crimes like murder, rape, or theft. Look closer, though, and we will see humans behind the decisions that cause the economy to tank, the job to suck, the utility bill to be so high, the check to bounce, the car to crash.

Seven billion people live on this planet, and every one of them has thousands of opportunities a day to make decisions that adversely affect others. Seven billion making thousands! Let's just say each one makes a thousand decisions a day. I think that's conservative, but let's run with that. In our world, 7,000,000,000,000 decisions are made *every day*. If one percent of those are bad decisions, think of the ramifications.

In the middle of this mess, God shows up. Someone is rescued. Someone is loved. Someone is healed. Someone is comforted. Someone is given an opportunity.

Every good and perfect gift is from above, coming down from the Father of Lights with whom there is no variation or shadow due to change.

—James 1:17

You might respond, "That isn't fair! You're giving God credit for all the good things people do!"

To which I would respond, "That isn't fair! You're blaming God for all the bad things people do!"

So, which is it? The earthly perspective will give credit to humans for all the good things and blame God for all the bad. The heavenly perspective will give credit to God for all the good things people do and blame people for all the bad. Which one is right?

Is there a God who can save the world? Is there a human who can save the world?

Jesus, God in the flesh, can save the world. This is the point of the Good News, that the heavenly perspective is the right one. Jesus is fully human and fully divine. He took the punishment for all the bad things people do and unleashed all the good a person can be, even giving us the Holy Spirit as a pledge that we can be greater than what people can be on their own. And if a bad thing does happen…

Blessed be the God and Father of our Lord Jesus Christ, the Father of mercies and God of all comfort, who comforts us in all our affliction, so that we may be able to

comfort those who are in any affliction, with the comfort
with which we ourselves are comforted by God.
— *2 Corinthians 1:3-4*

Bad things happen because so many people are trying to build their own kingdoms. They use power, money, sex, influence, violence, and whatever they can to be in control. Good things happen because God loves the people who are trying to build their own kingdoms and is trying to help them give up their paltry kingdom to be a part of the Kingdom of Heaven.

Me.

You.

That person who hurt you.

That person you hurt.

Then, when we swear allegiance to (put our faith in) Him to save us, He transforms us so that we are empowered to be the healing kind, not the hurting kind. Why does anything good happen at all? Because each one of us has a *pneuma*, a spirit, that resonates with the Holy Spirit, even when we don't understand Him. That part of us made in the image of God brings good to mankind. But we still have the flesh fighting us the whole way until someone can come along and put that flesh to death for us. So bad things happen.

But good happens, too. Praise God.

Most of the time, the good things don't make the news. Behind every terrible event, we find God bringing good out of it. We just have to look for it.

I'm thinking about this right now and wondering if some of you feel misrepresented. You aren't saying God is responsible, but you are saying God is negligent. Kind of like a parent who sees someone bullying their kid and yet does nothing about it.

Okay, follow this line of thinking with me. People do bad things, and we want God to either prevent them from doing it or punish them for doing it. If He sees someone bullying His kid, He should stop them.

So, what do you want from God if you are the bully? Mercy? Understanding? Second chances?

Please consider this. Not everyone does, but most people want to be good. They do bad things sometimes, but they don't want to be bad people. Like you and me. What do they probably want when they make a mistake? Mercy? Understanding? Second chances?

The way to make the world a better place is not by zapping the bad ones. If we were as honest about ourselves as we are about the "bad people" then we wouldn't have anyone left after said zapping. Sure, the world would be a better place because all of humanity would be zapped.

No, the way to make the world a better place is to encourage the good in people, give them an idea of what good looks like, forgive them for the bad they've done, and provide them a way to be transformed so that they only want to do the good.

Again, enter Jesus. Fully human, fully divine, offering forgiveness to those who will put their faith in (swear allegiance to) Him for rescue, for life, for good. Those bullies you point out—like you and me—need it badly.

DECISION TIME

To live this out, we need the power of the Holy Spirit speaking to our spirits so that our souls will align with the One who understands goodness best—Jesus. We are offered His sacrifice so that we can have a clean slate, offered His Way so that we can understand what a good life looks like, and offered eternity to live in the kind of world we always dreamed could exist.

The Kingdom of Heaven.

But we must choose the heavenly perspective, not the earthly, to receive it. We cannot just choose to agree with the facts. We must choose to follow Jesus because the facts draw us to Him. When we do, our personalities will remain, but our motivations will transform. Instead of worrying so much about me, me, me, I feel at peace with "me" and start living to introduce others to this peace.

Peace I leave with you; my peace I give to you. Not as the world gives do I give to you. Let not your hearts be troubled, neither let them be afraid.

— John 14:27

So let me lay it out for you.

- ***The Kingdom of Heaven is reclaiming earth through the life, death, and resurrection of Jesus Christ of Nazareth, God's only Son.*** He is the only one fully human, fully divine, who lived a sinless life and rose from the grave. He did this to bring the Kingdom of Heaven to us and asks us to consider how much He loves us. He is not the invader of our culture. He is the Reclaimer of what has always been His.

- ***We who repent of our sins…*** But we must rethink Who will lead our lives and how we will live. We must ask Him to transform us into what we were always meant to be.

- ***and give allegiance to Him…*** That requires that we put our faith not only in what He has done for us but in what He will continue to do for us if we follow Him.

- ***are forgiven…*** yes, all the things you've done to harm yourself, harm others, and break your relationship with God—not only before you knew better, but after as well.

- ***and empowered by the Holy Spirit…*** Our yes to Him is rewarded with the gift of a Power able to transform us into the person we were always hoping we could be. We are filled by Him with Power and Love, with His gifts and His fruit.

- ***to spread His influence…*** The gifts are given so that we may be emptied of the fruit to spread love and maintain self-control. All we need to do is walk in the

Spirit, filled by Him to be emptied for the sake of others (both those who are Already and Not Yet believers).

- *as we boldly follow Him.* With His help, we can be courageous as we live out a peace that passes all understanding if we guard our hearts with the truth of the Gospel and walk in the Spirit as Jesus walked.

Look, I know the phrase, "What Would Jesus Do?" has become a meme of sorts. But when Charles Sheldon wrote the book that first used the phrase, it rocked the Christian world. (The book is called *In His Steps*, by the way.) Why? Because it exposed us for the self-help believers we were, too focused on being better people—too focused on comforting the Already—to bother with sharing the Gospel with the Not Yets.

Take heart, Already, if you are one of these right now. God is not done with you.

Not Yet.

Live this out, brother, and sister, please. God wants to save your soul, grant you forgiveness, transform you into the best you, and reach others through you to do the same for them.

He just needs your faith (allegiance). Will you give it?

STRENGTH: Practical Gospel Faith

I'm a hands-on kind of guy.

Don't get me wrong—I'll research a thing to death before I decide to commit to it. Once I do, however, I can't just understand it in theory. Nope. Gotta get in there and do the thing to really learn it.

So much of what we do to follow Jesus happens in our hearts, souls, and heads, that I sometimes just want something physical to do to demonstrate what I am feeling and thinking. When Jesus told us to love the Lord our God with all our heart, soul, mind, and strength, He showed that He knew this about us.

We need to be active in what we believe or we won't believe it for long.

My fear as we begin this, however, is that some of us will get to this part and think, "Finally! Just tell me what to do!" I don't want to disappoint you but I'm going to, well, disappoint you. You'll find some things here, but the intention isn't to give a task list that allows us to check it off and say we're Christians now.

Everything that is presented in this portion of the book is meant to put our faith in action, *but they are not the faith in themselves.* That's an important distinction.

As I mentioned in the first book, I believe Jesus gave the perfect Sermon on the Mount to show us how we learn best. KNOW this to BE this to…

When I first discovered this pattern in His sermon, I finished the sentence with …DO this. Know, Be, Do. After teaching for a while, though, I realized that most people were just waiting for the Do. "Tell me what to do, Pastor, so I can please God."

So, I'll start there. Here's what you can do to please God: give your allegiance to Him.

Jesus had just fed five thousand men along with their women and children with just five loaves of bread and two fish. The people tried to make Him their king, but Jesus was not interested in an earthly kingdom. He disappeared in the night so that the crowd woke up the next day to find Him gone.

What could they do? Find Him! They realized He must have traveled across the sea, so they took some boats to Capernaum and found Him there teaching in the synagogue. The first thing they do is ask Jesus when He got there, but Jesus sees right through them.

Jesus answered them, "Truly, truly, I say to you, you are seeking Me, not because you saw signs, but because you ate your fill of the loaves."

— *John 6:26*

To quote a famous line from *Monty Python and The Holy Grail*, "You're not fooling anyone, you know." The people saw the miracle of God and all they could think about was the value of full bellies. Later, they mention the manna that God gave their ancestors in the wilderness after they escaped slavery in Egypt.

This wasn't any normal bread. Manna literally showed up with the dew of the morning and rotted if they tried to keep it overnight. Except for the manna on Fridays, that is. That manna lasted two days and was a double portion so the people would not have to gather any on the Sabbath (Saturday).

How much more miraculous can you get? Bread that just shows up on the ground in the right quantity, is good to eat, and has special expiration dates geared toward their religious lifestyle? You'd think they would be eternally grateful like the little green guys in *Toy Story* ("You saved our lives! We are eternally grateful!")

Interestingly, when God did that for the Jews, their response was not gratitude but boredom. Turns out boredom does something to memory cells, too, because they were suddenly able to recall all the fish and meat they had when they were in Egypt—completely impossible as slaves—and complained.

But now our strength is dried up, and there is nothing at all but this manna to look at."

— Numbers 11:6

Jesus knew providing an earthly kingdom would not lead to the Kingdom of Heaven. In fact, it would thwart that Kingdom. He was not interested in providing earthly bread for them when they had something much better available to them.

Do not work for the food that perishes, but for the food that endures to eternal life, which the Son of Man will give to you. For on Him God the Father has set His seal.
— John 6:27

The Jews thought they understood. Jesus had already provided some bread miraculously. Perhaps this was the bread He meant? Maybe He just wants to know they will work for that food and not expect it as a handout. So they asked Him what they must do to do the works of God. They wanted a checklist, a way to prove they were good enough to get what they wanted.

Jesus answered them, "This is the work of God, that you believe in Him Whom He has sent.
— John 6:29

Catch that? To believe in a set of facts would not have been much work. Most likely, if the Jews just had to give a mental nod to Jesus as king, they would not have complained. Who wouldn't want that deal? I say the right words, call Him the right title, and He gives me all I will ever need. Cool! *(This should sting a bit. Isn't that what we unintentionally teach people in the church today?)*

But we know after our time together that Jesus meant more than an agreement. He was asking them to give their allegiance to Him. The work they needed to do was to put their faith in (give allegiance to) Jesus as King of Heaven. Immediately, the conversation changed and the Jews wanted to know by what right He was declaring Himself that kind of King. And they expected signs (John 6:30) to prove it.

Listen to this lesson, sister, and brother. The work of God is to give your allegiance to His Son *because of what He has already done*, not because of anything else He will ever do. In the story John tells, all they had seen was a miracle meal. We have heard witnesses tell us Jesus lived a perfect life, died, and rose again to save our souls from our own sinfulness, impart the Holy Spirit to us fully, and send us to witness to others.

What would you do for a King like that?

WHAT HE HAS ALREADY DONE

Especially if He already proved His loyalty to you.

To feel the depth of His loyalty, we must remember the full extent of it. Let's walk in the shoes of first-century citizens and learn the way they did how much Jesus loves them. It shouldn't take long, but you know what they say: faster started, sooner over.

You're walking along the Jordan River and you hear a man in a camel hair suit speaking to a crowd. He's in the water with someone as he tells the crowd that he must prepare the way for the Messiah who is to come. Sternly, he shouts that we must all repent of (rethink) our lives and devote ourselves to God. Lovingly, he turns to the person next to him and asks for her repentance. She nods, tears in her eyes, and lets him lower her into the water. When he brings her back up, hers are happy tears. She wipes away the stress of the reality of who she is without God and vows to live for him from now on.

Some Pharisees show up and demand to know if the man thinks he is the Messiah. No, he does not claim that lofty title; but he says again he is preparing the way for the One Who is. You are intrigued and spend the day listening to him. Right before dinner, you decide you want a new reality. Going forward, you swear to your repentance (rethinking) and let the rough, callused hands put you under the water. As you come up, you rejoice that you have this new opportunity to learn what it means to devote yourself to God.

Taking the first step, you believe that your reality without God is lacking something. You rethink your life and decide to include God in it somehow.

The next day, you are still listening to this man named John—you think of him as the Baptist—and learning about following God more closely. Suddenly, John stops and points to another man and says, "Behold, the Lamb of God, Who takes away the sins of the world!"

The man doesn't look especially different, but you appreciate that the man walks to John, has a short conversation with him, then gets baptized, too. But that's when things get crazy. Later, you can't exactly describe what happened except to know that you heard a voice from heaven recognize this man Jesus as the Son of God. Some of John's people go with Jesus, but you've been away from your work for a few days and you have to get back to business.

Your next step is to recognize that some people believe Jesus is the way to God. Intrigued, you start to look into it.

Later at one of the great feasts, you see this same Jesus tell people He is the light of the world and that if people believe in Him, streams of living water will flow out of them. You ask a former fisherman named Andrew who seems to be close with Jesus. Andrew believes Jesus is the Messiah! You've heard about some of the miracles He supposedly did, but you haven't seen any yourself. While Jesus argues with some of the religious teachers, Andrew tells you about the healing, the casting out of demons, and the power over nature Jesus has expressed.

More than that, Andrew tells you about the life of Jesus and this sermon He did from the mountainside and how He called everyone to repentance and told them the Kingdom of Heaven is near. Excited, you go and tell some friends who also were baptized by John. Maybe this is the Messiah!

Turns out this Jesus guy is cool. He preaches love and grace most of the time and seems to prepare us for the idea that He is the way to fully understand God. Not sure if you buy it yet, but you are very curious.

But wait. He's been arrested for blasphemy? You can't get any details, so you go to a courtyard and hear Pilate declare the man is innocent. Yet the crowd screams to crucify Him. You can't bear to watch, but you make a decision that day. People need to hear about this preaching of Jesus and John the Baptist so they, too, can be devoted to God.

Jesus is crucified on a hill outside the city. You can't even bear to go see that, it's such an ugly scene. Wondering what the other disciples of John the Baptist are going to do, you gather with some of them. While Jesus is dying on the cross, you remember as a group how it felt when John the Baptist was beheaded. Rumor has it the disciples of Jesus are holed up somewhere, waiting. For what? Maybe for their turn to be arrested.

You've heard that Jesus died for our sins, but as you explore your next step you wonder how that is different from any other leader of a religion. It's great that Jesus proved His loyalty by dying for me. So what?

Then you hear that Jesus has risen from the grave.

Risen from the grave? How can that be? You don't believe it and go about your day until Pentecost. When you hear that the disciples of Jesus preached the Good News that Jesus has risen, you can tell by the way people respond that it is true. Your group of John's disciples decide that it's time to tell the world what has happened, so you leave everything behind and start traveling around sharing the story.

Today we don't have eyewitnesses and firsthand testimony. Oh, wait. Yes, we do. What we call "The Gospels" are the accounts of eyewitnesses and close partners with other eyewitnesses that this really happened. Jesus really rose from the grave, proving His loyalty to us in a way no one else ever has.

He didn't just die for us. He conquered death. Now, in His Kingdom of Heaven, Jesus is even King over death. You want to believe it, but you wonder what it will cost you.

One day, many years later, you end up in Ephesus and hear this man Apollos talking about Jesus. He says that Jesus is the Messiah and that we are to give our allegiance to Him. Much of His teaching has to do with the Kingdom of Heaven and how to take up your own cross and follow Jesus.

But how? You've been trying since John to be devoted to God and feel like it is a losing battle. You just don't have the willpower to do it. Confused, you gather with your group of John's disciples to talk about it. A man named Paul discovers you in that meeting and asks an interesting question about the Holy Spirit. You've never even heard of Him! Paul asks what baptism you have received and you declare your allegiance to Jesus, but that John baptized you.

And Paul said, "John baptized with the baptism of repentance, telling people to believe in the One Who was to come after him, that is, Jesus."

— *Acts 19:4*

You realize you need to give your full allegiance to this Jesus that John had foretold would take away the sins of the world. Baptized into Jesus, you receive the Holy Spirit and are empowered to give your full allegiance to Him. From that day forward, the Spirit shows you what it means to live in your reality with God. You are no longer alone to find out, and neither are your brother and sister disciples. Power to live for the Kingdom has been given to you.

Now you know it's not about what it will cost you. It's about what it cost Him.

THE LONG-AWAITED CONVERSATION

Over and over again, the first thing the King asks of His new followers is that they be baptized. This concept of baptism has been controversial in the church for almost as long as the practice has been established. Many great, learned men and women have studied the Bible and come to an array of conclusions.

Some believe baptism is being fully dunked in the water, others believe a sprinkling will do. Some believe the water saves you, others believe baptism isn't part of salvation at all. Is baptism a necessary part of salvation or is it the first step in obedience? Some believe being dunked in water isn't necessary at all, but a baptism of the Holy Spirit is necessary. Some believe the baptism of the Holy Spirit happens the same time we get dunked, others think it is a separate baptism that can happen before, during, or after.

The cleaning up of these arguments is beyond the scope of my book. But I will say this. Jesus was baptized. The disciples were baptized. The disciples baptized others. To baptize is part of the Great Commission (Matthew 28:19). Baptism by water figures prominently in The Acts of the Apostles. Baptism is often referred to by Paul, mentioned by Peter and John. When James says to be doers of the Word and not hearers only, is there any doubt then that baptism falls under it?

The argument about baptism shouldn't prevent us from being baptized. You may say the water doesn't save you. I agree with you, but…

Wait, I can't use that anymore.

The water doesn't save us, but the ritual cements our allegiance. Every king requires a ceremonial kneeling before him in a public setting to make us accountable for our oaths. Jesus does us one better. He has given us the example first, then asked us to participate in something that nowadays looks a whole lot like going down into the grave and rising again to new life.

In this ceremony, we are wed to Christ and His Kingdom in a way that publicly holds us accountable to our oath. I'll let the theologians fight over it from there, but maybe this illustration will make some sense to you. A marriage doesn't make two people love each other. They already do that without the ceremony. A marriage doesn't even secure the love for all time. The ceremony does three things for the couple:

1. They make their vows to each other before God's representative, a pastor or priest.
2. They make their vow to God before each other.
3. They make their vow before their families and friends to enlist their help in holding them accountable to love each other in any and all circumstances.

Months later when they are struggling because the husband leaves his socks on the floor and the wife puts on the toilet paper roll the wrong way, they can both point back to their vows and say, "On that day, I gave my allegiance to this sock-thrower/toilet-paper-ruiner. I said for better or worse."

In a way, baptism performs the same function in our allegiance to God. We are making a vow to God before God and before the people of God. It doesn't create our love for God, nor does it secure God's love for us. Yet it cements the allegiance we have to Him so that on those days when we are tempted to turn from Him, tempted to disobey Him, or have deliberately turned from Him and disobeyed, we can point back and say, "On that day, I gave my allegiance to this life-saver/sin-forgiver and He has promised to love me for better or worse."

Baptism is a beautiful rite, a sacrament, that ushers us into a relationship with God we can no longer deny. God and the people have heard where our allegiance lies. We do it to fully commit to Him. Let's argue about what part of the process it is *after* we've proven our allegiance in this way.

Fight me, theologians. I'm just kidding. I don't want to fight.

KINGDOM LIVING

Maybe you've come this far with me and wondered what I meant when I suggested that we had misinterpreted the message of the Gospel. Well, here we are. I believe we have been so inundated with the blessings from God in the Good News, we've either never heard, forgotten, or ignored the responsibilities (we tend to have a Grace-Only Gospel).

Those who have heard the responsibilities have preached the divine bait and switch. Sure, grace saves you, and what a wonderful gift that is. We can do nothing to earn it and we should be grateful for it. But now you have to follow the Law or else (we tend to have a Truth-Only gospel).

Grace-Only people come preaching blessings and Truth-Only people come preaching responsibilities. Jesus came preaching the Kingdom of Heaven is at hand.

But what is the Kingdom of Heaven?

This is also a controversial doctrine, though not as much as baptism is. I'm going to do the same with this controversy that I did with the first one—keep it simple. I don't intend to divulge a brand-new way of looking at this part of the Gospel. I'm happy just to get you thinking about it. Let's look at a couple of things Jesus said.

When Jesus was arrested in Gethsemane, He was eventually brought before the Roman government to be condemned to death. Pilate was the officer who could make that decision, but he didn't want to create a disturbance by passing judgment on an innocent man. The Jews accused Jesus of fomenting rebellion against Caesar and setting up a kingdom of His own. Pilate wanted to know if this was true. The answer Jesus gives him provides insight for us.

"My kingdom is not of this world. If My kingdom were of this world, My servants would have been fighting, that I might not be delivered over to the Jews. But My kingdom is not from this world."

— *John 18:36*

Just as he has throughout his entire account of the life of Jesus, John focuses on a difference between the earthly perspective and the heavenly perspective. The Jews were looking for a Messiah who would establish the Kingdom of Israel once more. By revealing Himself as Messiah, He opened the door for them to accuse Him of this. But this came from an earthly perspective of the mission of Christ.

Jesus disabuses us of this notion. The kingdom He came to establish is a heavenly one, not an earthly one. In another place, His words expand our understanding.

> *The Kingdom of God is not coming in ways that can be observed, nor will they say, 'Look, here it is!' or 'There!' for behold, the Kingdom of God is in the midst of you.*
>
> — *Luke 17:20-21*

Some will argue with me that this is a different kingdom. I'm just too simple, I guess. Who is the King of the Kingdom of Heaven? Jesus! Who is the King of the Kingdom of God? God! Who is Jesus? God! I don't see a need for God to set up a separate kingdom for His Son when they are also one and the same (as hard as that is to understand).

Jesus says we will never be able to see the Kingdom from an earthly perspective. It won't be Israel or America or anywhere else. No, this Kingdom is *in the midst* of us. Jesus rules in the midst of us, and yet it can't be seen. That sounds like something that must be seen from a heavenly perspective.

How can we become citizens of a kingdom we can't see? By giving allegiance to (putting faith in) the same King. How do we do that?

Repent, for the kingdom of heaven is at hand.
— *Matthew 4:17*

Truly I say to you, unless one is born again he cannot see the kingdom of God.

— *John 3:3*

Truly I say to you, unless one is born of water and the Spirit, he cannot enter the kingdom of God.

— *John 3:5*

As we start, we need to rethink (repent of) our lives so far and realize we have done many things that have hurt us, hurt others, and broken our relationship with God. That's the reality of who we are without God. We must be born again through the Spirit by giving our allegiance (faith) to Jesus who died and rose again to save us. When we do so, we are part of the Kingdom of Heaven. Our allegiance to (faith in) King Jesus the Savior, cemented by the ceremony of baptism, allows us to point to the day we joined that Kingdom and celebrate.

What blessings we receive! The power of the Holy Spirit to transform us, comfort us, direct us, convict us, move us to repentance when we fall. A group of people who will support us, spur us on to a better life, encourage us to improve ourselves. Eternal life.

Belonging to a Kingdom, however, also means falling under the rule of the King. Our allegiance (faith) means not just our willingness to accept Jesus as Savior, but to accept Him as Lord. How important was this idea to Jesus?

Have you ever heard the phrase "famous last words"? What someone says at the very end of their lives is important to us. When those words have wisdom in them, even more so, right? Well, what about the words of a man who died and rose again and spent forty more days on the earth with His disciples?

He presented Himself alive to them after His suffering by many proofs, appearing to them during forty days and speaking about the Kingdom of God.

— *Acts 1:3*

Kingdom of God, Kingdom of Heaven. This is what was so important to the resurrected Jesus. How do we honor that? Here are four simple steps to use your strength, your resources, for the sake of the King to whom you have sworn your allegiance.

But before I list them, I want you to think of these as responsibilities that are benefits. We don't *have* to do these things; we *get* to do these things. God made us partners (2 Peter 1:4) in His mission to expand the Kingdom of Heaven to the ends of the earth until we can say "God, you answered the prayer your Son taught us! Your Kingdom has come, Your will is done here as it is done there in heaven!"

We get to help Jesus bring "there" here. Not in some amazing way where sin ceases to exist, but through transformation —one person at a time—until the King comes to claim His own! The perfect culmination of this will be when Jesus comes back for us, but between now and then we are to strive to bring as many with us as we can.

One last suggestion as I name the four things we can do. Some of it can be done by ourselves, but most of it requires being with a group of like-minded believers. Because I'm writing to frustrated believers like myself, I suspect we will struggle with this. The church is the problem! How can the solution be inside the church!

Depends on your understanding of church.

The church of Jesus Christ is the problem, but *we* are the church. If I isolate myself from other believers, the enemy starts licking his chops. He's prowling around, you know, just waiting to catch believers alone and unprotected (1 Peter 5:8). Christianity is a very personal faith (allegiance), but it is not meant to be an individual faith (Hebrews 10:25).

I'm not saying you can't be saved unless you are in church. I am saying now that you have given your allegiance (faith) to Christ, you are the church. If the Body of Christ, the church, is sick, it's a matter of time before that sickness affects you. What can you do about it?

These four steps not only help you fulfill the Good News— they do so by blessing other allegiants (faithful) first. Paul was clear about this.

> *So then, as we have opportunity, let us do good to everyone, and especially to those who are of the household of God.*
> — *Galatians 6:10*

Maybe you've avoided "going to church" for a long while now, especially after the pandemic. I'm not suggesting you suck it up and go back to church yet. We will deal with that in a later book. God sees you already as part of the household of God and He is asking you to be part of the solution; or else you're just part of the problem.

As you read these four steps, I give you permission to find three brothers or sisters or a mix thereof to practice these together. You aren't starting a church; you're joining a movement of God. But do these things in His name for each other first, then see if He doesn't call you to further action.

ENGAGE

Right in the middle of His sermon, Jesus addresses the worry that drives many of us to sleepless nights and endless heartburn.

> *But seek first the Kingdom of God and His righteousness, and all these things will be added to you.*
> — *Matthew 6:33*

Before I realized how important the Kingdom is to Jesus, I struggled with this passage. How do I know when I've got this right? What does it mean to seek the Kingdom of God, and how does that relieve the worry Jesus addresses?

The root of that word "seek" is *zeteo* and Strong says it can mean to seek, desire, require, or demand. It's like looking for something, requiring evidence until you are sure. Ever felt that way? I have, and I usually say, "I'm going to get to the bottom of this."

Yeah. Get all the way to the bottom of it. I've knocked my car keys into the trash before (and right as I was already leaving late for an appointment!). Heard the *thunk* as they landed and the *clink* as they slid down through a couple of aluminum cans. Maybe I should have recycled so that less stuff was between me and what I needed so desperately.

I had to literally take pieces out of the garbage and set them aside so that I could get to the next layer. Could I stop? No, not if I wanted to get what I needed. So I peeled back the layers to get to the nugget down at the bottom. Then I grabbed the keys, put everything back, washed my hands (and the keys!), and ran for the door.

I couldn't go anywhere, though, until I engaged in the search and found what I sought.

In the same way, seek the Kingdom of Heaven. Where do you find it? In the Bible, of course, but not just there. Hold on, Alreadys, I'm not saying some truth is outside the Bible. I'm saying just as much heresy has come out of the Bible as truth when people have tackled it all by themselves. We need to ask the Spirit for understanding and gather with others who Already Believe if we really want to grab hold of the keys.

More than that, we need to discover the principles of the Kingdom and engage in them. Where can we do all those things? Only in a gathering of believers. That's why the writer of Hebrews (I believe it was Paul, but it doesn't matter) says:

And let us consider how to stir up one another to love and good works, not neglecting to meet together, as is the habit of some, but encouraging one another, and all the more as you see the Day drawing near.

— Hebrews 10:24-25

One of the trends sped up by the COVID-19 pandemic is Christians beginning to neglect meeting together. Don't get me wrong, I'm not talking about Sunday morning services (although most gatherings happen then). I'm talking about gathering with others who Already Believe in any capacity that promotes the Kingdom.

Why is this? My firm belief is that church leaders assumed most people understand the benefits and responsibilities of each person who gathers. We know what the Praise Team is supposed to do, what the preacher is supposed to do, what the children and youth leaders are supposed to do, and what the hospitality team is supposed to do. What is everyone else supposed to do?

Stir. Encourage. Serve. Live.

The word I came up with to describe all of that is *engage*. This is a byword among many church leaders today. They are more interested in how many people in their congregations are engaged than they are in how many attend. This is a good trend, but it requires new teaching for those who misunderstood.

Many have bought the lie that they can "have church" in their homes watching a livestream or checking out podcasts or catching the latest sermon from the most popular Christian superheroes of the day. I'm a big fan of Alistair Begg, Tony Evans, and many others.

This is going to hurt me as much as it might hurt you: When I get wisdom from them, I'm not engaging in the church. I'm selfishly filling my plate at the buffet and eating all I can eat. What happens if I do that too long without any exercise? I become unhealthy.

So the first thing I can do to seek the Kingdom of Heaven is to go where the Kingdom is already established and engage. Get aggressive about what it means to be in the Kingdom. Earnestly seek out even if I must go through garbage to find the keys.

> *From the days of John the Baptist until now the Kingdom of Heaven has suffered violence, and the violent take it by force.*
>
> — *Matthew 11:12*

Don't settle. Engage.

GIVE

I know the first thing we think about when we are asked to give is money. That's probably okay with God. After all, Jesus talked about our wealth as much as anything while He was here teaching about His kingdom. One of His heroes of the faith is the widow who gave all she had (Mark 12:44).

Does Jesus love money that much?
No, He loves your heart that much.

Do not lay up for yourselves treasures on earth, where moth and rust destroy and where thieves break in and steal, but lay up for yourselves treasures in heaven, where neither moth nor rust destroys and where thieves do not break in and steal. For where your treasure is, there your heart will be also.

— Matthew 6:19-21

This admonition is right in the heart of the Live portion of the Sermon on the Mount. Jesus knew our penchant to be selfish with everything we have—our time, our talent, our gifts, our resources, our money. He isn't really talking just about money here but using it as an illustration of everything because we base so much of our success on our wealth.

Yet even if we die with millions in the bank, eventually someone is going to squander it, something is going to destroy it, someone is going to steal it. He who dies with the most toys still dies. So what do they really matter?

This is an earthly perspective He is trying to cure in us. The heavenly perspective is to realize some things are more important than our wealth and status. If we choose then to use what we have for the sake of the Kingdom, our hearts and our treasure will be Kingdom-worthy.

Not only is this a better way; it is the right way, since we are stewards of what we've been given. Several of Jesus' parables bring this to light. We use them to teach about money often, but really it's about all our resources. Whatever resources we have are God's, on loan to us. The steward of the Kingdom is charged to do with the resources of the Kingdom what the King would do Himself.

So if I use my gifts for myself, that's not bad but not what's best. If I use my gifts for the Kingdom, I will find that I am sowing seeds and will reap a harvest worthy of the King.

The really cool theological stance to take lately is that the New Testament never explicitly states that we should tithe. For my Not Yets, "tithe" literally means "ten percent." Many Already Believers who have studied the Bible are starting to suggest that they *shouldn't* give the local church any money.

I have to agree the New Testament is vague on how much we should give. But I can't agree that we can take that to mean we shouldn't give. After all, Paul drew a direct correlation between sowing spiritual seeds to enlarge the Kingdom and the support he got from some of the churches.

> *If we have sown spiritual seed among you, is it too much for us to reap a material harvest from you?*
> — *1 Corinthians 9:11*

The reference seems clear to me. Paul is saying, "You received spiritual benefit from me. Is it too much for me to ask you to take care of my material needs?"

Someone will argue that I left out the next verse on purpose. Here it is:

If others have this right to your support, shouldn't we have it all the more? But we did not exercise this right. Instead, we put up with anything rather than hinder the gospel of Christ.

— 1 Corinthians 9:12

I didn't leave it out at first to avoid the argument, but to highlight a truth. Verse twelve doesn't negate verse eleven, it qualifies it. Paul is saying it should be expected that someone sowing spiritual seeds in us should be supported by us so they can be free to do it. Then he says in this one instance he chose not to take any material support from them because he believed it would hinder the Gospel.

In other words, Paul knew seasons where it was best for him to refuse the support so that the Good News would be free to spread. Yet he also had seasons where he was grateful for the support he received.

And you Philippians yourselves know that in the beginning of the Gospel, when I left Macedonia, no church entered into partnership with me in giving and receiving except you only.

— Philippians 4:15

Yes, Paul talks about learning to be content, but that doesn't negate what he is praising here. The Philippians believed so much in the Kingdom of Heaven that they wanted the Good News to be spread to all people. How could they do that? By resourcing Paul; so they did.

Too many churches and individual Christians have used Paul's Corinthian decision as an excuse to impoverish the pastors and leaders of their churches. This isn't what Paul meant. What he was describing was the urgency of the call and the reality that truly called preachers of the Good News will preach for free if that's what's necessary to spread the Kingdom.

Not that they always should, but that they should always be prepared to go without.

Giving is not just about money, though. When we serve, we give of our gifts, talents, compassion, mercy, and life. We let someone know they matter to God. Jesus wants to bless our efforts because He uses our efforts to prove Himself to others.

When the disciples James and John asked to be put on the right and left hands of Jesus, their Master disabused them of the honor of those positions. They wouldn't be positions of power but of suffering. Maybe if it had been an earthly kingdom, they could have ruled with Jesus, but in the Kingdom of Heaven, things would be different than the Gentile governments were.

> *"But it shall not be so among you. But whoever would be great among you must be your servant, and whoever would be first among you must be slave of all."*
> — *Mark 10:43-44*

What's all this got to do with you and me? Just this: giving is a natural outflow of the blessing of the Gospel in our lives. Jesus even told Paul it is more blessed to give than to receive (Acts 20:35). If a true seeker of the Kingdom wants to know what can be done to support the spread of the Kingdom, it can be summed up in one word.

Give.

Give your money so that someone can devote his or her life to finding out more and more truth about Jesus and teach it to as many as possible.

Give your time so that someone can come and receive when they don't have anything to give.

Give your gifts so that someone can see God's grace in your actions for them and wonder what they can do with their gifts to help someone else.

Give of your compassion and mercy so that others can heal and use that healing to give compassion and mercy to the next one who is hurting.

Give of your talents so that others can learn from you the truth of the Kingdom of God.

I hear someone explaining that right now they just can't give. Seasons come when giving is impossible, that's true. But they are seasons, not lifestyles. Come to get when you must, but think about this: If you come to get, you usually don't give. But if you come to give, you always get.

This is what it means to be part of the Kingdom. Engage. Give.

GROW

I've read the Parable of the Sower dozens of times, maybe even a hundred times over the years. Yet every so often I will feel like I've never seen the story before. This is one of those times. I didn't realize how much the Kingdom of God was involved in it!

When Jesus tells the parable, the disciples are confused and they ask Him what it means. He lets them know that the "secrets of the kingdom" are for them and not for the crowd. Why is that? I don't think Jesus was excluding the crowd from heaven, but I think He knew they were not yet ready for the impact of His teaching.

So when they ask, He lets the disciples know how blessed they are to get to hear the explanation. When He reveals the meaning, however, it's all about the Kingdom!

For those unfamiliar with the Parable of the Sower in Matthew 13:3-9, Jesus talks about a farmer scattering seeds on different kinds of ground. Some fall along the hard-packed path and birds come to eat it. Some fall on rocky ground where they sprout plants but have no roots and die. Some fall among thorns and are choked out. The rest fall on good soil and produce a crop that exceeds the expectations of the farmer.

What do these mean? We don't have to wonder because Jesus tells us. Notice how He couches the whole conversation as he explains what the first seed represents.

> *When anyone hears the word of the Kingdom and does not understand it, the evil one comes and snatches away*

what has been sown in his heart. This is what was sown along the path.

— Matthew 13:19

The seed is the word of the Kingdom. Some will not understand, so the word will not prompt the hearts of those people to put their faith in (give allegiance to) Jesus. If we are to be citizens of the Kingdom, we must be prepared to understand the words of the Kingdom.

The same word that is snatched away can also be received at first and then allowed to wither and die before it can take root (20-21). Not only that, but some can hear and understand the word of the Kingdom but decide to care more about what the world thinks than what the King thinks (22). Only those who understand the word of the Kingdom and take it to heart bring a harvest for the Kingdom.

As for what was sown on good soil, this is the one who hears the word and understands it. He indeed bears fruit and yields, in one case a hundredfold, in another sixty, and in another thirty.

— Matthew 13:23

This is a rich passage with many lessons, but let's just stick with the most obvious one. To be fruitful in the Kingdom is to understand and apply the word of the Kingdom. Can we do this with podcasts and live streams? Absolutely! Yay!

As long as we don't look too hard at that word "understand" in the passage. That word doesn't just mean to get it and be able to explain it. Instead, it promotes the idea of life application from it. We don't grow by learning more about the Bible. We grow by applying more of what we learn.

This touches on one of the frustrations I will deal with in a later volume, but I'm not afraid to take a moment to preface it here. Especially in the American Church, the Age of Reason has been a blessing to us in that we have become more diligent in our study of the Word of God. We want to accomplish what Paul suggested:

> *We destroy arguments and every lofty opinion raised against the knowledge of God, and take every thought captive to obey Christ, being ready to punish every disobedience, when your obedience is complete.*
>
> *— 2 Corinthians 10:5-6*

If we just knew the Word well enough, we believed, we could demolish all the arguments against the faith (allegiance) and people would have to believe in Jesus! I see three problems with this. I hope as I list them that you hear a plaintive heart, not a condemning heart. I'm not angry about it anymore. Instead, I am plaintive. My frustration doesn't make me shake a fist since I started rethinking (repenting of) my motivation to change the church. Instead, I approach this list tearfully, with a hope to convince out of love.

1. No one has ever been argued into the Kingdom of Heaven. Not even Jesus accomplished this. When the disciples wanted to know, He responded with "Come and see," not "Listen here." Yes, he argued with the Pharisees. It got Him crucified. He didn't argue with Nicodemus, He demonstrated God's love to Nicodemus—who, by the way, was saved.

2. This passage should be connected to the one before it, where it says our enemy is not flesh and blood (2 Corinthians 10:4). The arguments we are demolishing are the arguments of the Enemy, not arguments of the people we are trying to reach. We are saving them from the prince of the air, not proving them wrong for their sake.

3. Even if I am wrong about points 1 and 2, this point still trumps all. Did you notice in that passage our responsibility? In order to be successful, what did we have to do? Take captive every thought and *make our own obedience complete!*

To help the people of the world to see the truth of Jesus, we have to apply what we have learned in our own lives. When we take captive every thought, we can address the stinking thinking of others. When our obedience is complete, we can then be confident to approach the disobedience of others.

Instead of arguing people into the Kingdom, God is asking us to "example" them into the Kingdom. We need to know the

Word of God well, though, because as we imitate Christ we will act differently than everyone else. Inevitably they will ask why, and Peter tells us to always be prepared to give a reason for the hope we have (1 Peter 3:14-15). He also says to do that with gentleness and respect.

That means we can't just be a people of the Word. We have to be a people of the Person. The Word helps us understand the Person, the Person helps us understand how to live. When we live as the Person through our understanding of the Word, our light shines and we will have others ask us for the hope we have.

We have filled ourselves with knowledge, but we have forgotten that even the Word disagrees with the idea that knowledge is the endgame when 1 Corinthians 8:1b says, "Knowledge puffs up." What builds up? Love!

What's my point? I believe we get the most growth out of a plan that includes three phases:

Acquisition – I can't live in the reality of who I am with God until I know the reality of who I am with God. To do that, I have to acquire knowledge.

Application – I can't know the reality of who I am with God until I practice what I've learned. To do that, I have to be among people I can bless.

Accountability – Whether I like it or not, I can't guarantee that I will practice what I've learned unless someone is asking me about it and holding my feet to the fire.

Real growth comes from a process that includes all three steps. Part of giving my allegiance to (putting my faith in) Jesus is becoming ever more proficient at living under His authority. We fool ourselves into believing we can do this without anyone's help. What often happens, though, is that we start treating God as if He looks a whole lot like us.

I remember right after God called me into full-time ministry how nervous and excited I was. Really, I was a child playing with power tools. What is this? A drill? What does it do? I want to use it to cut this board! Oh, I need a power saw. I was hoping to use that to put some nails in that board over there.

Scared of doing everything wrong, I confessed to a fellow employee that I was lost. He suggested I call his pastor and talk to him, so I did. The pastor was courteous and asked questions about my calling and my life, my salvation journey, and my studies. Then he asked me a strange question.

"Son, this is important. Who is your pastor?"

"Oh," I replied, "we don't have a pastor at our church right now."

"Who is your pastor?"

"I guess I'm the closest thing to a pastor there."

"No, son. Who is your pastor?"

"I don't understand."

"Everyone needs a pastor. Even pastors. Mine is . . ."

I don't remember the rest of the conversation, but I do remember his point. He said to be without a mentor or pastor was to believe I had all the answers. Once I believed I had all the answers, I opened myself up to accidentally believing heresies that fit my own personal bias. He encouraged me to get a pastor so that I could avoid this pitfall.

I've had one since. To grow, you should have one, too.

The Kingdom can't be shaped by us, but the King loves to help us discover it. We do that best by reading His Word, praying, and listening to others who are further down the path than we are.

Engage. Give. Grow.

SHARE

This last is the endgame. The Good News is for each of us, but not only for us. We have to remember that our salvation is for us, but our sanctification is for them. When we engage and give and grow, we will supernaturally become better people. That isn't the goal, though.

Think about it, Not Yets. What I am presenting to you is the idea that God in His infinite wisdom knew we could not find peace and harmony and life without Him. Our sins—hurting ourselves, hurting others, and breaking our relationship with Him—separated us from Him. He responded by sending His Son to live a perfect life, die for us, and rise again as the King of Heaven and conqueror of death. Swearing our allegiance to (putting our faith in) Him makes us holy, gives us eternal life, and provides a clear path to reality with God.

Why doesn't He just take us to heaven right then? If He did, we wouldn't have time to mess up the holiness He gave us!

That doesn't seem to be His idea of success, though. More than just saving us from ourselves and making us holy, He reminds us of our new allegiance (faith) and calls on us to a process of . . . holiness. So we are holy, but we are becoming holy.

But we can't become "holier" than we are with Jesus, and in fact, we run the risk every minute we live with Him of mistakes, bad decisions, impulsive behaviors, misunderstandings, and returning to outright selfishness.

Why?

How were you reached for Him? Through the process of sanctification in others. They trusted Jesus as their King, gave Him their allegiance, and chose to engage, serve, and grow. More than that, someone decided to share what they experienced with you. Even this book is a process of my own sanctification with the hope of bringing you to accept Jesus as Savior and Lord.

Why did God choose to do it this way? I don't know. Considering how error-prone we are, it doesn't seem like a very good plan. Yet Jesus from the very beginning had just this plan. "You have seen me, now go and do likewise."

> *Heal the sick in it and say to them, "The Kingdom of God has come near to you."*
>
> — *Luke 10:9*

After watching Him do the healing, they were sent to heal. After watching Him proclaim the Kingdom, they were sent to proclaim the Kingdom. Jesus knew they would face adversity, so He wanted the disciples to remember their unwillingness to accept the Kingdom did not change the truth of the Kingdom's coming.

> *"But whenever you enter a town and they do not receive you, go into its streets and say, 'Even the dust of your town that cleans to our feet we wipe off against you. Nevertheless know this, that the Kingdom of God has come near.'"*
> — *Luke 10:10-11*

This sounds harsh, but the point is that belief or unbelief, allegiance or rebellion, faith or faithlessness, nothing changes the truth of the Good News. Because this is true, we need to make sure people understand what they are rejecting.

Jesus isn't a lifestyle choice.
Jesus isn't a comforting way to approach death.
Jesus isn't a human contrivance.
Jesus is the way, the truth, and the life (John 14:6).

How can we love God with all our strength? By being ambassadors of Good News for Him. Paul does a great job of making the case.

> *For the love of Christ controls us, because we have concluded this: that One has died for all, therefore all have died; and He died for all, that those who might live no*

longer live for themselves but for Him who for their sake died and was raised.

— 2 Corinthians 5:14-15

We are coming into this argument at its endpoint. We'll approach the entire argument he is making in a later volume. For now, live in these sentences for a bit. Please, if you will, read the verses again.

We are controlled—some versions say compelled—by Christ. This isn't a tool for exorcism to cast out a demon, Hollywood notwithstanding. This is a burning fire in Paul's soul that causes him to act in a certain way. Because King Jesus conquered death for him, he can't help but recognize the gift is available to everyone. If so, then someone has to tell them! He goes so far as to say he can't live for himself anymore because the Good News is too good to keep to himself.

From now on, therefore, we regard no one according to the flesh. Even though we once regarded Christ according to the flesh, we regard Him thus no longer. Therefore, if anyone is in Christ, he is a new creation. The old has passed away; behold, the new has come.

— 2 Corinthians 5:16-17

More than anything, the Good News has changed Paul's perspective from earthly to heavenly. He understands now that when he first encountered Jesus he thought of Him as a man.

That's why he was willing to persecute the church when he was named Saul (Acts 8). Now that he has seen Jesus as the divine Savior and Lord He is, he also sees the people around him through the same lens.

Not that they are divine themselves, but that they can be a part of the Kingdom of Heaven if only they believed in (gave allegiance to) Jesus. This is the King of kings and Lord of lords! He doesn't just reform our religious lifestyle, He transforms us into the "creatures" we were always meant to be!

> *All this is from God, who through Christ reconciled us to Himself and gave us the ministry of reconciliation; that is, in Christ God was reconciling the world to Himself, not counting their trespasses against them, and entrusting to us the message of reconciliation.*
> — *2 Corinthians 5:18-19*

To "reconcile" is to balance accounts. To make it all come out even, to perfect it. God didn't just do that for Paul. He did it for the world! And because He did, Paul can't help but share the message with everyone else. To keep the message hidden was to condemn people to a reality without God. Why would he do that?

Why would we?

I've heard people say, "I believe what I believe and I don't want to offend anybody by trying to make them believe what I believe." Don't we understand how utterly selfish that is? To withhold the message is to condemn those who don't hear.

I agree with you, Michael, but . . .

No, listen. This isn't debatable. This is the difference between today's version of belief and the Bible's version of faith (allegiance). If we really believe Jesus is the only way, then we will be compelled—controlled by it—to share Jesus with others.

Therefore, we are ambassadors for Christ, God making His appeal through us. We implore you on behalf of Christ, be reconciled to God. For our sake He made Him to be sin who knew no sin, so that in Him we might become the righteousness of God.

— *2 Corinthians 5:20-21*

Imagine being a first-century believer and reading this from Paul. Later, he comes to your town and you have a chance to take him to the side. You tell him, "Paul, I understand this is important to you, but you can't talk to people like this. It turns them off. They want to know how to raise their kids, be good spouses, and make it through a workday. Teach them topical things. You're good at that, you know."

Paul would quote Jesus as he stepped back from you. "Get behind me, Satan! For you are setting your mind not on the things of God, but on the things of man (Mark 8:33)."

Paul wouldn't be upset that you wanted to make better people, better parents, better spouses. He would be upset because you have asked him to be an ambassador of the good life when he has been called to be the ambassador of the Good News.

Good News! The Kingdom of Heaven is reclaiming earth through the life, death, and resurrection of Jesus Christ of Nazareth, God's only Son. We who repent of our sins and give allegiance to Him are forgiven and empowered by the Holy Spirit to spread His influence as we boldly follow in His footsteps.

The Good News brings the good life, but we should never confuse the two. Instead, we should hear how important the Good News of the Kingdom of Heaven is to King Jesus.

And Jesus said to him, "Leave the dead to bury their own dead. But as for you, go and proclaim the Kingdom of God."

— Luke 9:60

Giving our allegiance (faith) to the One who conquered death and sin for us means believing in Him for ourselves, engaging with other believers, giving our resources, growing in our faithful (allegiant) behavior, and sharing Him with as many as we can.

Engage. Give. Grow. Share. That's biblical faith.

Will you give your allegiance to Him?

The Next Step

Maybe you've had the same frustration about the salvation Jesus offers. You took His "free gift" and then got confused when you had to take transformational steps. That's not because Jesus pulled a bait and switch on you, but because somehow you missed the "Lord" part of the equation.

Someone might have told you and you didn't hear them. Someone might have twisted it up with making new believers look like the church people (Truth-only Gospel). Another might have been told what they did before and after didn't matter because Jesus forgives it all (Grace-only Gospel).

So let me say it plainly. Jesus is God and man, the only one ever, and He came to live a perfect life and conquer death and sin for us. All we have to do is believe in Him to receive the benefits He has to offer.

But to believe is not to agree. You must recognize His sovereignty and swear an oath to Him. That's what the "good confession" really is.

He said to them, "But who do you say that I am?" Simon Peter replied, "You are the Christ, the Son of the living God."

— Matthew 16:15-16

The Christ is the Anointed One, the King, and to be the Son of the living God is, in some amazing way, to be God Himself. We don't owe mental assent to Him; we owe allegiance.

When we give it, we receive benefits. Eternal life. Freedom from sin. Encouragement from fellowship. Transformation of character. These are all the benefits we already knew, but the extra benefits we've discovered are the responsibilities.

Engage. Give. Grow. Share.

These are not burdensome. In fact, as we incorporate the Lordship of Jesus in our understanding of the Savior Jesus, we begin to understand more fully what Jesus told His disciples.

"Come to me all who labor and are heavy laden, and I will give you rest. Take my yoke upon you, and learn from me, for I am gentle and lowly in heart, and you will find rest for your souls. For my yoke is easy, and my burden is light.

— Matthew 11:28-30

Stop trying to do it all on your own. Aren't you tired? Don't you want to put that weight down? Rest in Jesus and let Him show you how to live for Him. He's the Master, but He is good and He wants what is best for you in your life. Not only that, He wants to help you bless all the people in your life with His goodness lived out in you.

Know what that is?

Good News.

For Allegiant Rethinkers Only

Right out of high school, I took my alcoholism to the University of Evansville to study theater performance. Many good memories there. Met one of my future best friends there. Began my journey into sobriety. Performed on stage in the Kennedy Center in Washington, D.C. I met a girl I thought I might marry.

I knew acting would not support a family, so I started looking for a different way to make a living that appealed to me. Tried the idea of teaching English and Theater in high school, but it just didn't capture my imagination. Somebody suggested I take a survey of my life and ask myself what was most important to me.

God showed up in that process, but I didn't really listen to Him. Nope. Didn't want what He had to offer. As a confirmed atheist (really more of an agnostic), I liked trying to convince people to leave their faith. I wasn't interested in finding mine.

During my unofficial survey of the Life of Michael Rogers, I remembered my acting teachers telling me to spend my free time practicing expressions in the mirror and acting out different characters on visits to the local stores. Only once had I done that, preparing myself for a role as a blind man. That's a story for another time.

The memory convinced me that acting wasn't all that important to me. What was? Well, when I had free time, what did I spend it doing besides drinking?

Writing. Drunk or not, writing. Now that I was drunk a lot less, more writing.

I went to the library and found a couple of books on being an author and read them both in less than a week. Two lessons came from those books. The first one said he never read manuscripts from a person who was less than 35 years old. He convinced me to make it my goal to be published before I was that age.

Somewhere out there is a book called *Throwing Gazes to the East*. It's terrible, but it's proof of my victory. A small company published it for me when I was 31. Don't go looking for it. Really, really bad.

The other book taught me a different lesson. The author said not to go to school to learn how to write because the professors would "steal your voice." He said the best way to learn how to write was to write. Period.

I left school at the end of the semester. Gave up my full ride scholarship and started writing the Great American Novel. It still sits in my file cabinet to this day.

To make ends meet, I started driving pizzas for Dominos. That's where I met Geoff. He was a good guy, but he wasn't very bright. We used to tease him all the time, get him all riled up about something he knew was true until we convinced him it wasn't. Then we would admit what he had believed at first was true after all.

I needed Jesus.

We called him Gee-Off (hard 'g') just to upset him. I didn't know why he stayed friends with us back then, but I do today. Gee-Off was a follower of Jesus. Though he wasn't bright, he was persistent and he believed he could make a difference in our lives.

Often, I would question him on a point of Christianity that I thought proved it wasn't true. Surprisingly, I learned two things about Gee-Off. First, that he was more prepared about that topic than any other; second, that I couldn't shake his faith.

One night when we were sitting around having burnt pizza in my apartment (the boss had let us take it home), I approached what I thought was the final, winning argument. What follows here is not exactly how the conversation went, but it's close.

"Gee-Off, you believe in the Bible, right?"

"Yep. It's the Word of God."

"And doesn't that Bible say that your god is the same yesterday, today, and forever?"

"That's right."

"Then why don't you offer sacrifices like the Jews? Doesn't it have this whole religious system built on killing rams and goats and stuff?"

Gee-Off looked at me for a moment, but not out of confusion. I remember his eyes got wet and I didn't know why. He said, "You don't know?"

This was not how the conversation was supposed to go. "Know what?"

"We don't have to do that anymore because of Jesus." And in his halted speech and limited vocabulary, for the very first time someone shared the first steps of the Gospel with me.

If you have been reading with me so far, you know that it would be years later when I would give my allegiance to (put my faith in) Jesus. But right there, in that moment, I was confronted with a truth I couldn't argue around.

MAYBE NOT ALL AT ONCE

If you are Not Yet a believer, I hope this book has convinced you to put your faith in (give allegiance to) Jesus. Truly, my life has been blessed since I said yes to Him. Much of it I didn't understand until later, but the parts that made sense were enough to bless me as I learned. The more I heard God's voice and felt God's love, the greater the blessings until I realized even serving Him with all my heart, soul, mind, and strength was a blessing.

Maybe I'm your Gee-Off, and you don't know what to do with it yet. Okay. Salvation is a process, not an event. It happens, but maybe not all at once. I'm just glad you took this journey with us. If you are willing, walk the rest of this process with us as you explore what it means to follow Jesus.

What could it hurt? No one's asking you to move on it until you are ready. When you're ready, though, what follows will also help you decide what you should do about it next.

THEN AGAIN, MAYBE

Just maybe you have finished this book and gone from Not Yet a believer to one who Already Believes. Praise God! You will find what comes next even more helpful.

For those of you who are Already Believers now, I hope what you have read has prepared you to reconsider your level of faith (allegiance) and how you can explain it to a Not Yet. Look at the first half of what follows as opportunities to draw in the Not Yets in your life and ask them to consider where their allegiance (faith) lies. The second half is more of a challenge to rise up and renew your faith (allegiance).

Then again, maybe you are already doing that, too. The second half will still be valuable to you as you find Already Believers who are struggling with their allegiance and help them discover what biblical faith really is.

Gee-Off, wherever you are . . . thank you.

INTRODUCTION

1. What motivated you to read this book? Was your curiosity satisfied, or do you still have questions?

2. Before reading this book, what did you understand the Gospel to be?

3. Have you been so frustrated with the church that you've said hurtful things about her? Even if they were true things, were you speaking that truth out of a desire to heal her or hurt her?

4. If you are an Already Believer, do you have a simple way that you share the Gospel? Based on what you've heard in this book, will you make changes to it?

5. If you haven't been sharing the Good News, how has this book made it easier (or more difficult) for you to share?

KNOW – TENSION

Not Yet Believers

1. How do you feel about the Good News right now? Is that different than when you picked up this book?

2. What are your specific doubts about the Good News? What in detail is keeping you from saying yes to Jesus?

3. Doubts are often questions that haven't been answered yet. What would it take to clear those doubts?

4. Who would you trust to help you find those answers?

Already Believers

1. What is your Good News story? How did Jesus find you?
2. Think about your first few months as a believer. How were you encouraged to live out your faith?
3. Who was instrumental in discipling you? How did they do it?
4. What would you do differently if you were discipling younger you?
5. What area of your life has been the hardest to turn over to Jesus? Why?

KNOW – TEACHING

Not Yet Believers

1. How do you feel when someone tells you to "repent"? Does it help to understand it as "rethinking how you have lived your life"?
2. What does it mean to forgive? Would you describe it as an event or a process? Why?
3. How do you see God? What do you like about God? Dislike?
4. What do you think you would have to do differently in your life if you decided to believe in Jesus? Would that be a good thing, a bad thing, or a neutral thing?

5. Describe God. Describe Jesus. Describe the Holy Spirit. Share your description with someone who already believes and ask them to share what they think.

Already Believers

1. How often is the "Gospel of John the Baptist" given as the full Gospel in the churches in your area?
2. What is your definition of sin? Would you change your wording if you had to describe sin to someone who doesn't know the Bible?
3. How would you define the Kingdom of God? What kind of influence does the Kingdom have on your part of the world today?
4. In your area, what do most churches expect of new believers after they give their lives to Christ?
5. Is a godly life supposed to be exhausting? What does Jesus mean when He says He came to give us abundant life?
6. What part does the Holy Spirit play in your faith?

BE – BELIEVE

Not Yet Believers

1. Read one of the Gospels. I personally would choose John for you, but Mark is the shortest one. Keep a

notepad or make notes on your tablet that reminds you what you learn about Jesus as you do.

2. What surprised you about Jesus? What questions do you have about Him?

3. Has a church person hurt you somehow? Can you forgive them? Are you willing to separate how you feel about them from what you are learning about Jesus?

4. What evidence—I mean evidence that you can see to-day—do you need to put your faith in Jesus?

5. If Jesus really rose from the grave, is that enough? Why or why not?

Already Believers

1. Read one of the Gospels. Yeah, I'd recommend John for you, too, but any will do. Pay attention to how Jesus teaches His disciples. Does He have classes? Does He do field trips? How do the disciples learn what they learn?

2. What surprised you about Jesus' way of teaching? What questions do you have?

3. If someone asked you to provide evidence that your faith in Jesus was warranted, what would you list?

4. Is the cross enough for you? What expectations do you have for God?

BE – BECOME

Not Yet Believers

1. What is the reality of who you are now? Is there anything you would like to change?
2. What do you think would *have* to change if you experienced reality with God?
3. Why are you good to others? Do you ever treat others badly? Why?
4. Is there a part of your personality you are afraid of losing if you give your allegiance to Jesus? What is it, and why is it important to you?
5. When you think of godly people, what are the traits you admire? What traits do you despise?

Already Believers

1. What is the reality of who you were without God?
2. What is the reality of who you are with God? How is it different from when you were without Him?
3. What transformation is God asking you to go through right now?
4. If someone asks about your relationship with God, how do you prove you have one?
5. Who do you trust with your faith journey? Will you ask them to tell you what they think is your next step in following Jesus?

LIVE – HEART

Not Yet Believers

1. What steps have you taken in the past to be a better person (work out, eat better, stop an addiction, control anger, be more truthful, etc.)? Have you had great success each time?
2. Why do you think it is so hard for people to change?
3. Is it difficult to believe God wants what is best for you? How can He prove that to you?
4. Are you willing to admit that sometimes what is best for you requires change?

Already Believers

1. How has your faith helped you to become a better version of you in the last year?
2. Why do you think it is so hard for Christians to change?
3. Do you have a difficult time still thinking of yourself as a "new creation"? Why?
4. Have you experienced a Lazarus resurrection or a Jesus resurrection? What is the difference?

LIVE – SOUL

Not Yet Believers

1. What does right living look like to you? Do you always live up to your own expectations? How do you feel when you don't?
2. Are your expectations of yourself so different from the last six of the Ten Commandments (you can find them in Exodus 20:12-17)? What is the difference?
3. Is it fair to say you not only can't keep all of God's commandments, you can't keep your own "commandments" of what a good person is and does? Why or why not?
4. In some addiction recovery programs, people are encouraged to introduce themselves by their name and their addiction. If you had to introduce yourself by your name and your greatest weakness, what would it be?
5. What if saying yes to Jesus means *never* having to identify yourself by your weaknesses?

Already Believers

1. What is the difference between guilt and shame? Is it okay to feel guilty? Why?
2. As a believer, you know God forgives you for sin. Do you believe His grace also transforms your nature so

that sin is foreign to you? What difference would it make if you did?

3. What part does the Holy Spirit play in your daily walk with Jesus?

4. What does it mean to have your identity in Christ? Is that given to you, or do you have to work for it? Explain.

5. In what part of your life are you screaming at the Spirit, "I can't want it!"

LIVE – MIND

Not Yet Believers

1. What part of deciding to put your faith in Jesus makes you want to say, "I agree with you, but..."?

2. Do you have an unanswered prayer in your past that has made it harder for you to believe in Jesus?

3. Which kind are you, glass half-empty or half-full? How does this affect your outlook on faith? On life? What is the shortcoming of your perspective?

4. Is there a right way to use money? Power? Sex? Influence? How do you know when you are doing it right?

5. Are you willing to consider the possibility that you don't always know what is right? What are the consequences if you are wrong? Who can you trust to tell you what is right?

6. Will you let Jesus show you what is right and how wrong you and I are at times; tell you the consequence of our wrong thoughts, actions, words, is death? Will you believe He fixed that by conquering death for you? Will you consider trusting Him?

Already Believers

1. What part of your life of faith in Jesus makes you want to say, "I agree with you, but…"
2. Do you currently have unanswered prayers that make it more difficult to put your full faith in Jesus?
3. How does God affect the way you view money? Power? Sex? Influence?
4. Describe the difference between an earthly perspective of the world and a heavenly perspective.
5. Are you ready to accept the mission to share what you believe with others?

LIVE – STRENGTH

1. Will you rethink (repent of) who you have been without God and ask Him to help you become who you can be with Him?

   a. If you've already done this, do you feel a need to do it again?

2. Will you give allegiance to Jesus as the King of kings and Lord of lords?

   a. If you've already done this, ask yourself if you have been faithful to that declaration in the last month. What would have to change for your allegiance to be meaningful?

3. Will you prove your allegiance to Christ by asking a church leader to help you get baptized?

   a. If you've already done this, don't feel like you have to do it again. If you sense that you gave mental assent to Jesus but not allegiance, sometimes it helps to recommit this way. Not necessary, but helpful.

4. Will you give allegiance to Christ and engage with other believers?

   a. If you are still leery of Sunday morning church services, don't let this keep you from engaging with believers. Start a group. Join a group. More than one other person, so that it requires more communication and cooperation.

   b. Interestingly, if you skip Sunday morning and have your own group, you're going to find how difficult it is to gather with people and avoid conflict. Don't let this force you to disengage. The conflict is where you're going to learn the most if it is done in Power and Love and Self-control.

5. Will you give allegiance to the King and be His steward of the things He gives you?

   a. Your time – will you devote ten percent of your time to serving others as you engage with those who Already Believe and those who are Not Yet Believers?

   b. Your talent/gift – will you do what comes naturally to you for the sake of others so that the King can bless them with your offering? What can you give? Don't be surprised if this costs you something.

   c. Your money – yeah, even that. Give some to a local church you believe is trying to really share the Gospel. Give some to ministries or charities that are serving the least of us.

   d. Your possessions – this is harder, actually. How can you use what you have so that people praise God for you having them?

   e. Your heart – I didn't lead with this on purpose. I wanted you to feel how hard all those gifts will be before reminding you that it's impossible to give anything else until you give your heart to him.

6. Will you live out your allegiance to Jesus by promising to diligently seek growth in your understanding, your application, and your accountability?

   a. Find good teachers and groups that will clarify what it means to follow Jesus.

b. Try to apply what you learn soon after you learn it.

c. Ask someone to ask you if you applied what you learned. Be honest with them.

d. If someone asks you to check on them, do it with encouraging words and not judgmental words. If they fail, fail them forward instead of pushing them backward.

7. Will you share with others your allegiance to Jesus and the reasons you chose to let Him be King in your life?

a. Even if you just said yes to Him, you know more than someone else about it.

b. If you said yes years ago but never established the practice, think about how you would tell someone these three things:

i. Before you knew Jesus, what was your reality without God?

ii. How did Jesus find you?

iii. After you said yes to Jesus, what is your new reality with God?

VOLUME THREE

By now you may be guessing the progression of this series. We start with ourselves so that we're prepared to hear all the truth about Jesus. Even as we finish learning how Jesus affects us personally, though, we are prompted to go outside ourselves to fulfill what he is doing inside us.

We are filled to be emptied.

The Holy Spirit intends to clean house in us, remind us who we are, empower us to be more. But not for us. Once we make Jesus King of our lives, we are guaranteed perfection in the end.

That means our salvation is for us, but everything else will be for the people around us—even as it benefits us as well. Let me remind you of the disciples' calling after Jesus proclaimed the Kingdom of Heaven was at hand.

> *And Jesus said to them, "Follow me, and I will make you become fishers of men."*
>
> *— Mark 1:17*

Just as Peter and Andrew left their nets immediately, King Jesus is asking us to immediately drop whatever we thought was most important and start thinking about how to make disciples. We took the time to *Rethink* and now we have learned to *Follow*. Are you ready to *Make*?

Join me.

Even if it gets a little frustrating.

Author Bio

Jesus-follower, husband, father of four, disciple-maker, and content creator, Michael S. Rogers is a veteran church leader, a frustrated but faithful follower, and a believer in the power of transformation for individuals and for the church.

Other Books
by Michael S. Rogers

Rethink: We love Jesus, no question about that. Church? Frustrating sometimes, isn't it? We know gathering with other believers is important, but many of us are suffering from PTSD: Post-Traumatic Sanctuary Disorder. Is there a practical path forward for frustrated believers both outside and inside the structure of today's church? What motivates us to pursue a revival of the mission we have been given?

Passing Lincoln: When her great-grandson returns the five-dollar bill with her note that he can trust God, Dolores is ready to give up hope. She wants to believe God can reach him, but she doesn't know how to help. Desperately, she puts her gift in the offering plate on Sunday morning and prays, "God, if you're really there, you can use my money to save one of those kids. I don't want to be selfish. It doesn't have to be my Little Chet. Whoever it is, God, I pray you use my gift to help them see Jesus." From wallet to purse to dumpster to pocket, her gift travels all over Beulah, Indiana, until it returns to the hands of the young man who gave it away. Passing Lincoln is a modern-day speculation of what God can do with a widow's two coins (Mark 12:41-44).

Will Changers (series):

Dark Forces Rising (book 1): The will of God has always been set in stone until now. Rick Walters knew that his life was meant for something greater, but he had no idea just how great it could actually be. Praymar, an angel of God, has joined with Rick, empowering him with God's light and strength, revealing a world beyond the limits of Rick's understanding. With Praymar's help, he can mend the destructive ways of the church, unifying them under God's glory and light. As he falls in love with Christine Feldman, a close friend and local lawyer in the small town of Marquette, Ohio, Rick begins to realize just how important each and every choice is. Together, with help from heaven, Rick and Christine struggle to rescue their embattled church from collapse. But their close friends have a secret, one that will open their eyes to a world beyond the realm of human understanding, a world of heavenly angels and sinister demons; a world of sacrifice, betrayal, and death, and of those who would change God's will for good and evil purposes. Hell is on its way to Marquette. As the darkness closes around each of them, Rick's greatest choice could be his very last. Dark Forces Rising, the first novel in the Will Changer Series, exposes the ultimate spiritual battle raging with all of us: If you had the power to manipulate God's will would you?

Unholy Trinty (book 2): The struggle between good and evil continues in the second novel of the Will Changers Series. Surviving the near-death encounters of hell's dark agents in the small town of Marquette, Ohio, Christine Feldman and Ryan Claymore battle the dark forces that have surrounded them. With the church broken and God's will tested, Christine and Ryan must turn to one another and the dim light of the angels to protect them. But the darkness is growing, closing in all around them and revealing a terrible new enemy that threatens to destroy Marquette. Will the Will Changers survive the onslaught? Can they save the church from the growing menace? Or will evil finally triumph? Twists, turns and shocking revelations answer these questions and more, as the saga of the Will Changers continues in book 2, the Unholy Trinity!

Wisdom Beyond His Years (e-book only): Isn't responsibility the strongest word you've ever heard? No laughter there. No fun at all. When my son Elijah was born, I was pretty sure my days of being a kid were over. I was responsible for teaching him about life, about God, and about being a man. God must have been laughing when He heard me worry over it. He knew what I didn't--that I would learn as much about being a child of God from my son as I would teach him. Responsibility doesn't necessarily mean growing up, but it does mean growing.